Cadette

Girl Scout

Handbook

Girl Scouts of the U.S.A.

420 Fifth Avenue

New York, N.Y. 10018-2702

GIRL SCOUTS OF THE U.S.A.®

B. LaRae Orullian, *National President*

Mary Rose Main, *National Executive Director*

Credits

Project Coordinator
Toni Eubanks

Authors
Toni Eubanks
Harriet S. Mosatche, Ph.D.
Rosemarie Cryan
Chris Bergerson

Contributors
Patricia J. Paddock
Donna Nye
Linda Fallo-Mitchell, Ph.D.
Sharon Woods Hussey
Martha Jo Dennison, Ed.D.
Maria Garcia
Judy Brucia

Editor
Janet Lombardi

GSUSA expresses appreciation
for the hundreds of poems and
quotations received from Girl
Scouts all over the country.

Design and Production
Kaeser and Wilson Design Ltd.

Illustration
Kevin Bapp, pages 16, 21, 26, 39,
58, 60, 68, 70, 71, 88, 91, 94, 97,
99, 100, 102, 106, 113, 115
Lisa Halter, digital illustration

Photography
Bachrach Photographers, page 100
Richard Blinkoff, pages 14, 15
Will Bond, page 117
Judy Griesedieck, pages 20, 40
John D. Hesselbein, page 7
Ameen Howrani, pages 17, 39
Alan Kaplan Studio, cover, pages 5,
23, 45, 65, 85 (left), 107, 125
Lane Brothers, page 6
Tim Rhoad, page 24
Rex Wilson, page 85 (right)

Photographs submitted by
Children's Defense Fund, page 9
Angela Frasure and Tina Edholm,
Central Kansas Council of Girl
Scouts (Kansas), page 19
Shelley Girshick, Girl Scout Council
of Greater New York (New York),
page 27
Juliette Gordon Low Girl Scout
National Center, page 28
GSUSA Archives and Photo Library,
pages 6, 8, 9, 10, 106
Barbara Harris, Northern Oakland
County Girl Scout Council
(Michigan), page 18
Alison D. Rappaport, Chesapeake Bay
Girl Scout Council (Delaware),
page 77
U.N. photo 182000/M. Grant Doc
1016L, page 41
Katherine Waszak, Girl Scout
Council of Greater New York
(New York), page 30

The attributed poetry and quotations that appear in this handbook were submitted by Girl Scout members as original work. GSUSA claims no responsibility for the origin of this material. Inquiries related to the *Cadette Girl Scout Handbook* should be directed to Membership and Program, Girl Scouts of the U.S.A., 420 Fifth Avenue, New York, N.Y. 10018-2702.

© 1995 by Girl Scouts of the United States of America

All rights reserved

First Impression 1995

Printed in the United States of America

ISBN 0-88441-283-0

10   9   8   7   6   5   4   3   2

This book is printed on recyclable paper.

CONTENTS

INTRODUCTION

Welcome to the world of Cadette Girl Scouting! It is an exciting, challenging world that offers new opportunities to learn about yourself and the world around you. Your handbook will help you explore personal interests, develop a healthy way of life, work on leadership skills, and provide service to your community.

HOW TO USE YOUR CADETTE GIRL SCOUT HANDBOOK

Each chapter of the *Cadette Girl Scout Handbook* covers topics of interest to Cadette Girl Scouts. The chapters also include activities, career descriptions, and sections marked "To Consider" and "For Discussion."

You may find it helpful to think of your *Cadette Girl Scout Handbook* as an idea bank and reference tool. This handbook can help you tailor your Girl Scout activities to match your interests and lifestyle.

You can also use your *Cadette Girl Scout Handbook* as a reference tool in exploring the recognitions available to Cadette Girl Scouts. Chapter 7 provides details on planning and preparing for recognition work.

In addition to the *Cadette Girl Scout Handbook*, don't forget that other Girl Scout books such as *Cadette and Senior Girl Scout Interest Projects*, *Ceremonies in Girl Scouting*, and *Outdoor Education in Girl Scouting* can help with recognition work as well.

FITTING IT ALL IN

You might ask: "How can I possibly participate in my favorite Girl Scout activities and pursue my other interests too? There just isn't enough time!" Many girls today have tremendous demands on their time: schoolwork, being with friends, after-school sports—just to name a few. But Girl Scouting can be a part of all of this. The key is to find ways of making Girl Scouts a part of the things you already do. Think about which interests correspond to your Girl Scout activities. Then plunge right in and enjoy your own special experience in the world of Cadette Girl Scouting!

Minutes From A Gathering Of Girl Scouts

Another Friday,
together, munching and laughing,
talking to my friends,
who I see only this one day.
We catch up on the week's events,
telling each other the setbacks
and the victories,
letting out stress before the weekend,
reassuring that bad times would soon be gone,
as we shout and giggle like we've always done.
Ten years have passed,
but still we gather in a familiar room,
to embark on adventures
through worlds unexplored.

–Hilary Kaplan, age 16,
Angeles Girl Scout Council, California

GIRL SCOUTING'S ROOTS AND TRADITIONS

Chapter 1

TAKING A LOOK BACK AT THE GIRL SCOUTS

The Garden Badge, introduced in 1931

You are a contemporary Girl Scout living in a world where much has changed since Girl Scout founder Juliette Low's time. You may feel disconnected from that world of the early twentieth century—before computer science, CDs, answering machines, VCRs, and microwave ovens. But as a Girl Scout, you are rooted in the same philosophy and values by which the early Girl Scouts lived.

The Girl Scout tradition connects you to the generations of girls who came before you, and to the girls who will follow you. What hasn't changed much over the years is the need for personal development and community service. Community service projects (see page 129) have helped generations of Girl Scouts develop self-esteem, clarify personal values, and feel pride in working with others toward a common goal. Which projects and activities did girls your age participate in during the early years of Girl Scouting? Many of them weren't much different from what you do today. Take a look.

1920s

A 1923 issue of *Girl Scout Leader* magazine mentions that girls helped pack and deliver holiday baskets for the Salvation Army. And like girls today, they enjoyed outdoor activities that had to "harmonize with our government conservation program." At the Eastern Conference for Camp Leaders in 1923, Girl Scouts were discouraged from collecting wild flowers and ferns or "mutilating trees in the pursuit of nature study." (Does that strike a familiar note?) Girl Scouts also participated in a Cleaner Brooklyn, N.Y., Parade on May 16, 1925, as part of an effort, along with the Brooklyn Chamber of Commerce, to clean up the city.

1930s

A new badge, the Garden Badge, was introduced in 1931. Girls had to make a garden 12 feet by 15 feet, and care for it for an entire season. A *Girl Scout Leader* magazine article mentions that girls benefited from "wise planning, steady, painstaking effort toward a

counter negative propaganda about the United States and were sent to "unknown friends" in Great Britain. Girls also made supplies for soldiers such as wooden shower sandals (there was a shortage of rubber), drawstring bags for personal items, and scrapbooks with news stories, cartoons, and quizzes. Since there was a loss of hospital personnel to the armed forces, Girl Scouts became hospital volunteers doing everything from telling stories to children and mending rubber gloves, to operating the switchboard.

definite goal, and the joy of accomplishment." During this decade, however, GSUSA began losing some of its teenagers. It was suggested that to keep teens involved in Girl Scouting, adults had to give them opportunities to develop leadership and management skills.

1950s

Girl Scouts continued their volunteer work in hospitals, libraries, and museums. They baby-sat while parents voted and attended PTA meetings. They made stuffed dolls for a children's home, held car washes to earn money, and collected books for the needy. In Omaha, Nebraska, in 1957, Brownie Girl Scout Troop 400 became special friends to a three-year-old girl who was deaf. Girl Scouts of Troop 50 in Ogden, Utah, gave a Halloween party at the state school for children with hearing and visual impairments.

1940s

During World War II, Girl Scouts were especially helpful to the war effort. They helped the United Nations by making scrapbooks that depicted daily life in America. These were needed to

JULIETTE LOW:
A LIFE WORTH HONORING

On a blustery February day in 1912, a middle-aged Juliette Low paced back and forth across the deck of the S.S. *Arcadian* on her return trip to America across the Atlantic. She was bringing home an idea that, for the time being, rested only in her imagination. That idea matured into a movement for girls "...of Savannah, all America, and all the world." It became the Girl Scout movement.

Juliette Low's achievement of bringing Girl Scouting to America was the result of her life experiences. Growing up in a large family, attending private school away from home, and living outside the United States led her to the idea of an all-girl movement for girls of her country.

Juliette Low (top center) with her brothers and sisters

JULIETTE LOW AS A TEENAGER

Daisy (as Juliette was called by her friends and family) spent most of her teenage years in boarding schools, first at a school in Virginia conducted by the granddaughters of Thomas Jefferson, then at a French school for American girls operated by two French women in New York City. Each day the girls dressed like French girls their age, in black aprons to keep their dresses clean. They walked two by two up Madison Avenue for their escorted afternoon walk. The girls often pleaded to be allowed to walk along Fifth Avenue—where all the boys were—but the school mistresses refused. They didn't allow the girls to have boys call on them, escort them, or even speak to them on the streets.

One time, during art class, Daisy's teacher noticed that she was sketching. The teacher thought Daisy was drawing a Greek temple, so she asked her to show the sketch to the class. Daisy did, but it wasn't a sketch of a Greek temple. It was a sketch of the teacher's oversized shoes, which she always wore, but had that day mistakenly put on the wrong feet!

JULIETTE LOW AS FOUNDER

Juliette Low was 52 when she returned home on that ship from England. Her health was not good; she had a severe hearing impairment, and she had never done any large-scale public work in her life. She was absent-minded, changeable, unbusinesslike, and seldom on time since she insisted on wearing her favorite watch even though it had only the minute hand intact. In some ways, she seemed like the least likely personality to undertake the founding of a national organization. Thankfully, Juliette Low felt otherwise and became busy getting things done and putting her goals for girls into action. However, by 1916, Juliette found that she could no longer personally handle the financial needs of the organization. It was time to bring on more supporters.

Juliette in authentic Japanese dress, 1887.

That's when she created a National Board. Today, the National Board has an active role in the running of Girl Scouts of the U.S.A.

Juliette with her sisters Eleanor (center) and Mabel (left).

Marian Wright Edelman is another woman who founded an organization that supports children. Known as the "children's crusader," Edelman, in 1973, founded the Children's Defense Fund, an organization that aims to teach the nation about the needs of children.

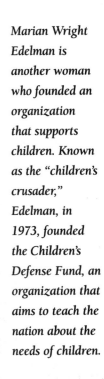

The Role of
Girl Scouts of the U.S.A.

GSUSA directs and coordinates the Girl Scout movement in the United States. National headquarters is located at 420 Fifth Avenue in New York City. There, the business of running a national organization and serving its three million members is conducted by over 400 employees.

Headquarters staff are involved in a variety of important and interesting projects. They write innovative handbooks, plan workshops, maintain

▲ TO CONSIDER:

If you were to found a new organization, what type of organization or business would it be? What would its mission be?

GIRL SCOUTS OF THE U.S.A.

membership data files, collaborate with outside agencies such as science museums and publishing companies, and perform other jobs that bring the Girl Scout experience to all girls.

One of the most important priorities of the national organization is to grant charters to local Girl Scout councils. A charter authorizes a council to make Girl Scout program available within a designated geographic region, like your own hometown. Delegates from each council attend a National Council Session every three years. This body elects the members of the National Board of Directors and determines general policy for matters affecting all Girl Scouts throughout the United States.

THE GIRL SCOUT PROMISE AND LAW

When Juliette Low returned to America to start the Girl Scout movement, she brought the English version of the Girl Scout Promise because she felt it was an oath that girls would understand. The concept of a "three-part Promise" can be clearly understood by the youngest Girl Scout: Girl Scouts are responsible to (1) their own spiritual beliefs; (2) other people; (3) the Girl Scout Law. The three-part Promise is symbolized on the World Trefoil pin (see page 15).

The 1913 version of the Girl Scout Promise reads:

Each girl must promise on her honor to try to do three things:

1. To do your duty to God and to your country.

2. To help other people at all times.

3. To obey the Laws of the Scouts.

Compare the 1913 version with the current version:

The Girl Scout Promise (Current)

On my honor, I will try:

To serve God and my country,

To help people at all times,

And to live by the Girl Scout Law.

THE USE OF "GOD" IN THE PROMISE

The word "God" in the Promise has always been used to represent the spiritual foundation of the Girl Scout movement. Since Girl Scouting is for all girls, girls whose beliefs are expressed by a word or phrase other than "God" may substitute that for the word "God" when they say the Girl Scout Promise. When written, the word "God" is always in the Promise.

The Girl Scout Law

I will do my best:

· to be honest

· to be fair

· to help where I am needed

· to be cheerful

· to be friendly and considerate

· to be a sister to every Girl Scout

· to respect authority

· to use resources wisely

· to protect and improve the world around me

· to show respect for myself and others through my words and actions.

Used thoughtfully and often in your everyday life, the Promise and Law can help you take action when you are faced with a decision. They can help you define or articulate the personal values that will give meaning and direction to your life.

"At their first meeting…each one should have a note-book, pencil, and a yard of cord, and they are taught the Scouts' Promise."

–Juliette Low

How Girls Can Help Their Country

ACHIEVING PLURALISM THROUGH THE FOUR PROGRAM GOALS

To live together happily in a country as diverse as America, members of the society need to take pride in their own cultural heritages while developing understanding, respect, and appreciation for the cultures, races, and religions of others.

The American ideal is to become a pluralistic society. In a pluralistic society, people of different backgrounds live and work in harmony, joined by the common bond of being citizens of the United States. Valuing human life in all its diversity is at the core of pluralism. Living, working, planning, and solving problems together bring us closer to a pluralistic society.

Diversity is like a mosaic of people of different sizes, shapes, colors, ages, religions, genders, and abilities who fit together side by side. Pluralism, however, is like a kaleidoscope where these differences interact with one another, form relationships, and become changed for the better.

The steps toward pluralism follow the four Girl Scout program goals for girls:

1 DEVELOPING SELF-POTENTIAL

Pluralism Goal:
To develop pride in one's own cultural heritage.

Suggestion:
Share part of your culture with your troop or group through games, crafts, customs, stories, etc.

2 RELATING TO OTHERS

Pluralism Goal:
To encourage understanding and appreciation of people from all cultures, races, and religions.

Suggestion:
Check your local library for good multicultural picture books and recordings for younger girls. Work with Daisy or Brownie Girl Scouts on multicultural activities and storytelling.

3 DEVELOPING VALUES

Pluralism Goal:
To promote actions and decisions that show a respect for all people.

Suggestion:
Be a positive role model in your words and behavior. Do not allow name-calling or behavior that excludes others.

4 CONTRIBUTING TO SOCIETY

Pluralism Goal:
To work in cooperation with others for the community benefit—especially in ways that eliminate discrimination and promote diverse people working or playing together.

Suggestion:
Become involved in service projects with other Girl Scout troops.

GIRL SCOUTS OF THE U.S.A. INSIGNIA AND UNIFORM

As a Girl Scout, you are entitled to wear the Girl Scouts of the U.S.A. membership pin in either the traditional or contemporary styles. These pins show that you belong to Girl Scouts in the United States. The membership pin with the eagle, in use since 1912, depicts the American eagle and shield, which are parts of the Great Seal of the United States of America. They symbolize strength, victory, self-reliance, peace, and might. The membership pin with the three girls' profiles, introduced in 1980, depicts three faces. The faces represent Girl Scouts and the value of diversity in Girl Scouting. Both pins symbolize your continuing commitment to the three-part Promise.

The Cadette Girl Scout uniform shows outwardly that you are a part of the Girl Scout movement. Wearing the uniform makes the organization visible

membership pin with the eagle

membership pin with three girl's profiles

to the public. This is especially important during special ceremonies and community service, and when traveling or participating in special events. Uniforms also help members identify one another and create a feeling of unity among them. Styles, fabrics, and colors are periodically updated based on girls' preferences. However, Girl Scouts are not required to own or wear a uniform.

THE WORLD TREFOIL PIN

Girl Scouts also wear the World Trefoil pin, showing that they are a part of an international movement. The trefoil used on this pin is a unifying symbol of the World Association of Girl Guides and Girl Scouts (WAGGGS). The three leaves represent the three-fold Promise, and the two stars represent the Promise and Law.

World Trefoil pin

WORLD ASSOCIATION OF GIRL GUIDES AND GIRL SCOUTS (WAGGGS)

Girl Scouts of the U.S.A. is one of 128 organizations worldwide that are members of the World Association of Girl Guides and Girl Scouts (WAGGGS). As a Girl Scout of the U.S.A., you are one of a family of 8.5 million Girl Scouts and Girl Guides the world over. Juliette Low and many women like her worked closely with Robert Baden-Powell, the founder of the Boy Scout movement. His sister Agnes and his wife Olave, along with Juliette Low, were strong forces in expanding Scouting and Guiding around the world. The spirit of the WAGGGS movement is channeled into several areas: self-development, teamwork through the patrol system, community service, outdoor activities, and partnerships between youth and adults. Through those avenues, young people like yourself experience moral, physical, and intellectual growth.

THE FOUR WORLD CENTERS

The World Association owns four world centers: Our Chalet in Switzerland, Pax Lodge in England, Our Cabaña in Mexico, and Sangam in India. The international gatherings and trainings held there are open to girls and adults from any of the WAGGGS member organizations. The world centers have been popular sites for international wider opportunities (see Chapter 2).

Career Focus

ENVIRONMENTALIST

What would I do?
You would work to create a balance between the needs of the environment and the needs of industry. You might specialize in such areas as land conservation, toxic-waste removal, acid rain, or wildlife preservation. As a consultant, you might study an industry's impact on the environment. As an activist, you might work with the community to pressure government or industry to change their actions.

Where would I work?
Much of your work would be done in an office, although you'd have to travel to different sites.

What skills and education/training would I need?
You'd need to be observant and have good problem-solving and communication skills. A college degree in environmental or political science is the minimum requirement. Many environmentalists start out as volunteers or interns.

Interest Patch Link: Eco-Action; Leadership; Wildlife; Energy Awareness.

USA GIRL SCOUTS OVERSEAS

Many Americans spend time living abroad. Girls whose families have been temporarily transferred to sites in foreign countries can maintain their Girl Scout links by joining American troops or groups in another country. Likewise, girls who have never been Girl Scouts but would like to join when they journey abroad may also do so.

Young women involved in Girl Scouting overseas enjoy various activities including those designed to further understanding of the culture of their host countries. A USA Girl Scout Overseas might share events with local Girl Guide troops and get to experience what the World Association of Girl Guides and Girl Scouts is really all about.

GIRL SCOUT/GIRL GUIDE TRADITIONS

Girl Scouts and Girl Guides share many symbols and customs. They enable girls from different countries and cultures to communicate with each other in familiar, comfortable ways.

The Girl Scout Sign

You show the Girl Scout sign or the salute by raising the middle three fingers on the right hand with the little finger held down by the thumb. This sign is used whenever Girl Scouts or Girl Guides recite the Promise.

The Girl Scout Handshake

Girl Scouts and Girl Guides all around the world use the handshake as another form of greeting. Girls extend their left hand, denoting friendliness and loyalty, while they raise their right hand in the Girl Scout sign or salute.

The Friendship Circle

Girl Scouts and Girl Guides often form a friendship circle in a meeting or at a campsite. Everyone stands in a circle, and each person crosses her right arm over her left, clasping hands with her friends on both sides. Each person is silent as a friendship squeeze is passed from hand to hand. The friendship circle stands for an unbroken chain of friendship with Girl Scouts and Girl Guides around the world.

The Girl Scout Slogan and Motto

Girl Scouts and Girl Guides everywhere have the same slogan and motto. The slogan, "Do a Good Turn Daily," has been in use since 1912. Girl Scouts of that era were to tie a knot in their neckerchiefs. The knot could not be untied until a good deed was accomplished. Before they went to sleep at night, girls were to think of the good deed they did that day. Today, the slogan is a reminder of the many ways, both large and small, that girls can contribute to the lives of others.

KEEPING THE PROMISE

"On my honor" *is how I've learned to live,*
So that I can earn trust from my companions.
I have been educated in this honesty
And my time and dedication is the return gift I give.
"I will try," *as I have done my best to*
help my organization grow,
To promote the values I have learned
By recruiting and teaching other girls
So that one day the same love I have, in them will show.
"To serve God and my country" *is*
another idea I have done
By teaching blessings and graces at meetings.
I have also journeyed to other places and countries
Serving and helping others, but my duty has just begun.
"To help people at all times" *and the needy*
I try to serve
By doing community service projects.
Saving the environment will also
help our people to live longer
So we camp and play with little
impact—our planet to preserve.
All of these things together, none can be withdrawn,
Make up my life and personality.
This is the organization most important to me,
So I serve it and **"live by the Girl Scout law."**

—Kaela Sáenz, age 18,
San Jacinto Girl Scouts, Texas

The motto, "Be Prepared," has also been in use since the early days of Girl Scouting. Girl Scouts during the early twentieth century learned skills not just for fun and satisfaction, but because they might need to cope with emergencies of that era. During the World War II years, Girl Scouts helped many citizens.

Today, so many people need help in communities all over the world. The motto reminds girls to prepare themselves to give service to others, and to lead full, productive lives as citizens of America and the world. Girl Scout service projects (see pages 129–130) are important ways you can contribute to the lives of others.

CEREMONIES

Ceremonies play an important part in Girl Scouting and are used to help celebrate special occasions, such as the welcoming of new members to your troop or group, the presentation of awards, or the Girl Scout birthday. Ceremonies can open or close a meeting, and may be short or long, formal or informal. Ceremonies may include girls in your troop or group, other girls in Girl Scouting, Girl Scout leaders or other adults, and special guests such as parents, relatives, and friends. They can be held by large groups or small groups, in the outdoors or indoors, and can include anything you choose. For more about ceremonies and ceremonial procedures, refer to *Ceremonies in Girl Scouting*.

The Format of the Ceremony

No matter what kind of ceremony you are having, good planning is essential so that the ceremony will be meaningful. Basically, a ceremony has three parts— the opening, the main part, and the closing.

The *opening* part of the ceremony can be used to welcome guests, tell the purpose of the ceremony, and set the mood for the occasion. For example, it might be quiet, festive, or serious.

The *main* or *central* part of the ceremony focuses on the purpose of the ceremony, the reason you have gathered people together. The focus might include singing songs, reading poems or choral readings, performing dramatics, or sharing candle lighting.

The *closing* part of the ceremony may summarize the ceremony. It might include forming a friendship circle, saying good-bye or thank-you to special guests, or singing a closing song.

Types of Ceremonies

Below are some ceremonies especially important in Girl Scouting:

• An *investiture ceremony* is held to welcome someone into Girl Scouting for the first time.

• A *bridging ceremony* is held when you "cross the bridge" to the next level in Girl Scouting.

• A *rededication ceremony* is held at special times when Girl Scouts want to renew their Girl Scout Promise and

review what the Girl Scout Law means to them. Troops or groups usually hold a rededication ceremony at the beginning and end of each troop year. A Girl Scout member can take part in many rededication ceremonies.

• A *Court of Awards ceremony* is one at which girls receive recognitions they have earned.

• A *Girl Scouts' Own* is a special ceremony created by a troop or group around a theme.

Candlelight and flag ceremonies, described below, are often used as part of larger ceremonies, but they can also take place on their own.

Candlelight Ceremonies

Candlelight ceremonies help girls to think about the meaning of the Girl Scout Promise and Law. Three large candles represent the three parts of the Promise, and ten smaller candles represent the ten parts of the Law.

Flag Ceremonies

A flag ceremony honors the American flag as the symbol of our country. As part of a flag ceremony, you say the Pledge of Allegiance. You might also sing "The Star-Spangled Banner" or another song honoring this country, such as "God Bless America" or "America the Beautiful." To conduct a flag ceremony:

1. The troop or group forms a horseshoe. The color guard is in position. All stand at attention.

2. The Girl Scout-in-charge says: "Color guard, advance." This signals the color guard to advance to the flags, salute the American flag, and pick the flags up. Then they turn together and get into position facing the troop. Everyone stands at attention.

3. The color guard walks forward carrying the flags to the formation. They stop in front of the standards.

4. The Girl Scout-in-charge says: "Girl Scouts, honor the flag of your country." The group salutes the American flag.

5. The Girl Scout-in-charge says: "Girl Scouts, recite the Pledge of Allegiance." This may be followed by songs, poems, or verses.

6. The Girl Scout-in-charge says: "Color guard, post the colors." This signals the color bearers to place the flags in their stands. They remain at attention next to the flags.

If the flag ceremony is part of a larger ceremony such as an investiture, the Girl Scout-in-charge commands the color guard to retire the colors by taking the flags to their places of storage. She can use any of the following commands:

"Girl Scouts, attention."

"Color guard, advance."

"Color guard, honor your flag."

"Color guard, retire the colors."

"Color guard, dismissed."

"Girl Scouts, dismissed."

IMPORTANT GIRL SCOUT DAYS

In every Girl Scout and Girl Guide country, February 22 is observed as a special day known as Thinking Day. It is the birthday of Robert, Lord Baden-Powell, who founded the Boy Scout movement in England, and his wife Olave, Lady Baden-Powell who continued the work of heading the Girl Guiding movement. On this day, Girl Guides and Girl Scouts make a special effort to exchange greetings with their sisters in other countries, and to give contributions to the Thinking Day Fund. This fund is used to promote the Girl Guide/Girl Scout organizations throughout the world.

March 12, the anniversary of the day when Juliette Low formed the first troop of Girl Scouts in this country, is celebrated as the Girl Scout birthday. The week in which March 12 falls is designated as Girl Scout Week.

Each year Girl Scout troops and groups across the U.S.A. honor Juliette Low on

FIRE FIGHTER

Career Focus

What would I do?
You would work to prevent fires by educating the public and inspecting buildings. Of course, if fires do occur, you would rescue people and extinguish the fire. You might also be called to help in other emergency situations: people trapped inside a damaged car, people suffering from heart attacks, or people in danger of drowning.

Where would I work?
You could work in any town or city, or in specialized locations such as national parks. Regardless of your locale, you would spend some time at the firehouse, some time in the community educating people and inspecting buildings, and some time at the emergency site.

What skills and education/training would I need?
You would need a great deal of stamina and strength to handle equipment as well as rescue people. You need to work as a member of a team, and be able to think quickly and clearly under pressure. You should earn a high-school diploma and be able to pass a civil service test and physical exam.

Interest Patch Link:
Emergency Preparedness; Outdoor Survival.

her birthday, October 31, by planning a variety of ceremonies and projects.

You can find ideas for special ceremonies for these occasions in *Ceremonies in Girl Scouting*.

As a Cadette Girl Scout, you follow in a long line of teenage girls who've shared laughter, fun, and learning with their sister Girl Scouts. Now it's your turn to carry on the Girl Scout tradition!

THE JULIETTE LOW WORLD FRIENDSHIP FUND

Started in 1929, two years after Juliette Low's death, the Juliette Low World Friendship Fund was established to honor Juliette Low and her vision of worldwide friendship. Every year, Girl Scouts throughout the United States give money to this fund, usually on her birthday, October 31, or on Thinking Day, February 22 (the birthday of Olave Baden-Powell and Robert Baden-Powell). The fund is used to promote international friendship and travel to the four world centers.

"My very first Wider Op was really special. I traveled on a plane for the very first time. Everyone acted like I was a 'big' girl going off on my own to experience the world. Being the fourth child of five, I was always called 'the baby.' Then, as that [plane] door opened for me, I was introduced to a whole new world of experiences and Girl Scouts became 'cool,' not something I wanted to hide my face from."

–Noelle Dry, age 15,
Rolling Hills Girl Scout Council,
New Jersey

WIDER OPPORTUNITIES AND LEADERSHIP

Chapter 2

Wider opportunities are experiences that go beyond the troop or group setting. Wider opportunities help broaden your horizons through meeting new people, traveling to different places, and doing new activities. Each year a number of wider opportunities with nationwide participation are sponsored by councils or GSUSA. They range from environmental projects in the north woods of Michigan to work with people with disabilities in California, and many, many other opportunities. Even if you've never traveled far from home before, there is bound to be a national or international wider opportunity to interest you.

Wider opportunities can be sponsored and operated by one or more troops or groups, a neighborhood group, a council, GSUSA, Girl Guide associations, the WAGGGS centers, or by community, national, or international organizations that work with Girl Guides and Girl Scouts. Wider opportunities can include non-Girl Scouts and community organizations as well as Girl Scouts and Girl Guides from different countries.

HOW TO PARTICIPATE IN A WIDER OPPORTUNITY

There are several ways to be involved in a wider opportunity. Whether you are a participant or part of the planning team, you'll find great rewards.

Some wider opportunities close to home might be:

• One troop invites another to participate in a film festival.

• One troop or group joins another to plan a trip to the state capital.

• Several troops or groups join in a project to make a park trail accessible for people with disabilities.

• A troop or group works with a senior citizen community center to put on a performance with senior citizens.

• Girl Scouts in the neighborhood hold an international festival, inviting community members to participate.

• A council sponsors a councilwide sports event for all Girl Scouts.

• Two neighboring councils bring together Girl Scouts to attend a statewide leadership conference.

Widening Circles

Girl Scout Experiences Beyond the Troop or Group Setting

WIDER OPPORTUNITIES WITHIN THE COUNCIL

Attended by: Girls within the council, and sometimes girls from neighboring councils.

Sponsored by: A troop, a neighborhood, or the council. Examples: troop trips, intertroop projects, ceremonies, neighborhood events, service projects, courses (such as first aid, arts, skating), interest groups, weekend events, troop camp, core camp, summer camp, traveling troops (within the United States).

WIDER OPPORTUNITIES WITH NATIONWIDE PARTICIPATION

Attended by: Girls nationwide, and sometimes international participants.

Sponsored by: A council and held at camps, colleges, conference centers. Examples: high-adventure outdoor events, service/career exploration events, arts events, events focusing on current affairs or global issues.

INTERNATIONAL WIDER OPPORTUNITIES

Attended by: U.S.A. Girl Scouts and Girl Scouts/Girl Guides.

Sponsored by: A troop, a neighborhood, or a council. Examples: trips abroad, trips to WAGGGS world centers (Our Cabaña, Our Chalet, Sangam, Pax Lodge).

Sponsored by: GSUSA (financed by the Juliette Low World Friendship Fund). Examples: international events in the U.S.A.; delegations to international encampments, conferences, community development projects, "home visits," WAGGGS-sponsored special events; international visitors to councils in special "council-designed" projects; international participants in council-sponsored wider opportunities with nationwide participation; international participants in GSUSA-sponsored events.

International Wider Opportunities

Wider Opportunities With Nationwide Participation

Wider Opportunities Within the Council

Some wider opportunities away from home might be:

• A council somewhere in the United States sponsors an event open to Girl Scouts throughout the country.

• A traveling Girl Scout group relives the turn of the century in the American South by visiting the birthplace of Juliette Low in Savannah, Georgia.

• Girl Scouts of the U.S.A. sponsors an international event and selects U.S.A. Girl Scouts to participate in an encampment. The event may take place in Europe, Asia, Africa, South America, or some other part of North America.

• A troop or group visits one of WAGGGS's world centers.

FINDING OUT ABOUT WIDER OPPORTUNITIES

Wider Opportunities Within the Council

Find out about local opportunities by talking to Girl Scout friends, your leader, and your council representatives. Look for notices on bulletin

---

Career Focus

TOUR ESCORT

What would I do?
You would accompany groups of people on organized trips, making them feel comfortable in an unknown environment. You would oversee the transportation, housing, and activities of travelers and be the person responsible for their safety. You would spend your day engaged in the same activities as the tourists.

Where would I work?
You could work for a tour agency and might be placed in a foreign city, at an archaeological dig, on a mountain range, or aboard a cruise ship.

What skills and education/training would I need?
You would need exceptional planning and organizational skills, along with the ability to interact well with different people. A high-school diploma is the minimum requirement, though some colleges offer degrees in tourism. Fluency in a foreign language or any specialized knowledge that would apply to a tour group (like art, history, and anthropology) would also be an asset.

Interest Patch Link:
Travel; Emergency Preparedness; Global Understanding.

---

boards or fliers at troop or group meetings or at school. Sometimes newsletters and special notices are sent to all registered Cadette and Senior Girl Scouts. Some councils even announce opportunities on radio or cable television.

Wider Opportunities with Nationwide Participation

Each year, Girl Scout councils in many parts of the country sponsor wider opportunities and invite Girl Scouts from across the United States to apply. These events are called "Wider Opportunities with Nationwide Participation." Girl Scouts of the U.S.A. may also sponsor opportunities at its national centers and elsewhere. Girl Guides/Girl Scouts from other countries are often invited to attend these events. This gives U.S.A. girls the

opportunity to meet their international sister Girl Guides/Girl Scouts.

Girl Scouts of the U.S.A. also sponsors international opportunities and selects Cadette and Senior Girl Scouts to participate in international encampments, conferences, community development projects, "home visits," and WAGGGS-sponsored special events in countries around the world.

The locations of opportunities with nationwide participation and the types of activities vary from year to year. You can find detailed information about these opportunities in *Wider Ops: Girl Scout Wider Opportunities*, a GSUSA annual publication mailed to all Cadette and Senior Girl Scouts each summer. It describes events, costs, locations, dates, requirements, qualifications, and financial aid.

I AM THE FLAME

I am the flame,

fighting to burn.

The strong gusts of wind,

stab at me in turn.

I'm growing weak,

from forcing my light.

But I will not die,

I'll try to be bright.

I bite and I lash,

defending my light.

I burn the wind,

It shrinks back in fright.

I've gained respect.

the wind has backed down.

My light I reflect,

to many a town.

I am the flame

shining my light.

Guiding my family,

throughout the night.

I am the flame

. grown since that night.

My family is all,

one can see in my light.

I am the moon

now old and wise.

A brilliant lantern,

that glows in the skies.

—Stephanie Tallett, age 14,
Tejas Girl Scout Council, Texas

The Juliette Gordon Low Girl Scout National Center

The birthplace of the founder of Girl Scouting in the United States is a registered national historic landmark in Savannah, Georgia. Cadette Girl Scouts enjoy visiting the former home of Juliette Low, which has been restored and furnished in 1870s style, to learn more about her and her family, her work with Girl Scouts, and life in the nineteenth century. To learn more, write to the Juliette Gordon Low Girl Scout National Center, P.O. Box 8044, Savannah, GA 31412-8044.

Edith Macy Conference Center

Edith Macy Conference Center, located 35 miles north of New York City on a 269-acre site in Briarcliff Manor, N.Y., is a year-round educational facility for Girl Scout adults. It also offers some events for girls ages 13–18. Adults in Girl Scouting may also come to the Creedon Center, a smaller conference center on the property of Edith Macy Conference Center. Nearby at Camp Andree Clark, traveling troops may camp on almost 200 acres of wooded hills.

Here are some other activities that can help you and your troop or group learn more about wider opportunities:

▲ ACTIVITIES:

1. Organize a wider opportunity information day for your troop or group and invite family members to attend. Collect information on wider opportunities and invite former wider opportunities participants to share the highlights of their experiences.

2. Interview former wider opportunities participants, then write a newsletter for your troop or group and/or neighborhood telling what you have learned from the interviews.

3. Design posters and fliers that would advertise a wider opportunity offered by your group, neighborhood, council, or even an event listed in *Wider Ops*.

WHO ATTENDS WIDER OPPORTUNITIES?

To make sure that participants have a successful experience, many times the sponsor of a wider opportunity requests that applicants have certain qualifications.

Participants must:

• Be registered Girl Scouts.

• Be interested in developing leadership skills.

• Be able to interact with girls from different racial, economic, and ethnic backgrounds.

• Be able to spend three days away from home.

A girl is selected to attend a wider opportunity with nationwide participation by the sponsor of the event. Primarily, girls are selected based on the requirements of the event and the number of participants each event can accommodate. Event sponsors try to select participants from different parts of the country so that everyone attending has a chance to meet Girl Scouts from other regions. Sponsors also try to select girls who have never attended a wider opportunity before and girls who are experienced wider opportunity participants. Finally, sponsors make sure that they have girls of various ages and school grades.

The *Wider Ops* catalog lists a variety of opportunities. To increase your chances of being able to attend, there is a selection process known as "Operation Second Chance." The application form has spaces for you to list three choices. If you aren't selected for your first choice, you may be selected for your second or third choice. Be sure to fill out the form completely.

HOW MUCH DOES IT COST?

The cost of a wider opportunity depends on the type of activities, the accommodations, the length of the event, and the location.

Opportunities within your council are most likely the least expensive. They may be free of charge, or cost anywhere from $10 for meals to $100 or more if overnight accommodations are needed.

Opportunities with nationwide participation will probably be more expensive. With the help of your family and your Girl Scout council, you are generally expected to pay the event fee and for transportation to and from the event.

Ways to Cover the Cost

Many Girl Scout troops and groups carry out money-earning activities to help girls pay for the cost of their wider opportunity. Before you plan a money-earning activity, check with your leader and your council. These opportunities are announced well in advance so that you can plan ways to earn money. Consider jobs such as baby-sitting or dog-walking.

Girl Scout councils often have special funds to assist girls who are selected to attend wider opportunities. In addition, "travelships" for wider opportunities with nationwide participation are available through GSUSA. Contact your council for further information on these special scholarships.

Finally, Girl Scouts of the U.S.A. also provides financial help for girls selected to participate in GSUSA-sponsored international opportunities.

THE APPLICATION PROCESS

Applying for an Opportunity with Nationwide Participation

Filling out the application is an important step in the selection process. Be sure to follow instructions and fill out the form completely and as neatly as possible. Parents, family members, Girl Scout leaders, and teachers can all be a great help, especially in obtaining references.

Once you've completed an application, make a copy of it. You can refer to it when completing future applications or when applying for other events.

Girls are usually interviewed by their council as part of the application process. It's one way to make certain the right person is selected for the right event. This is an important step in helping others to know you.

When you are applying for a wider opportunity, remember that both your Girl Scout and non-Girl Scout experiences and skills count, no matter how large or small they seem to you. Your ability to handle yourself away from home and with people from different backgrounds is extremely important, as well as your interest in the opportunity and the skills you can bring to the event.

Applying for International Opportunities

Each year, Girl Scouts of the U.S.A. receives invitations from Girl Guides and Girl Scouts around the world to send girls and adults to special events in their countries. The invitations can be for national or international encampments, community service projects, home visits, or events at the world centers.

When you apply for an international opportunity, you are not applying for a special event in a specific place. If and when you are selected, you will be given full information about the location and nature of the international wider opportunity, and you'll have time to prepare for your trip.

Participants in international opportunities are selected because they:

• Demonstrate an interest in international events.

• Are emotionally mature.

• Are flexible in coping with unexpected situations.

• Show an ability to deal with group living and are accepting of cultural and ethnic differences.

A council interview, council endorsement of your application form, and two references are also required. A national task group meets each year to make the selections for international opportunities.

OTHER INTERNATIONAL WIDER OPPORTUNITIES IN GIRL SCOUTING

International Post Box

Girls who are 10 to 17 years old can request a pen pal from Girl Scouts of the U.S.A. through the International Post Box. You need to get a special application form from your Girl Scout council. You must use this form; otherwise, your request will not be considered.

Fill out the form very neatly, in ink, and send it to Girl Scout national headquarters. (The address is on the form.) Staff members at national headquarters will then try to link you with a pen pal. Sometimes it just isn't possible to find pen pals for everyone. If you are one of the lucky girls who does get a pen pal, it may not be for at least six months; but the wait will be worth it, because many Girl Scout/Girl Guide pen pals correspond for years and become lifelong friends. However, if you don't receive a pen pal within a year of applying, you should reapply.

Traveling Troops, Groups, and Individuals

Many Cadette Girl Scouts individually and in troops or groups have visited Our Cabaña (Cuernavaca, Mexico), Pax Lodge (London, England), Our Chalet (Adelboden, Switzerland), and Sangam (Pune, India). All of the world centers have their doors open welcoming traveling Girl Scouts and Girl Guides. Girls may attend sessions at the center or may visit at any time during the year when regular meetings or sessions are not in progress there. Such visits should, of course, be planned well in advance.

Here's what one former Girl Scout troop did before traveling to Our Cabaña. Ms. Gruber's troop indicated to her that they wanted to travel to Our Cabaña. It sounded like a good idea so the troop investigated how to do this. After speaking to a representative at their council, Troop #1863 found out that:

• As soon as there is interest in traveling outside the United States, girls and leaders should inform the council and get permission to plan the trip.

• The chapter entitled "Planning Trips with Girl Scouts," in *Safety-Wise*, contains the basic information on how to plan such a trip.

• The procedures for traveling abroad, including visiting, obtaining accommodations, and taking part in current activities at a world center or a Girl Scout/Girl Guide headquarters, can be obtained through the council or through the Membership and Program cluster, GSUSA.

• The troop should *not* directly contact Girl Guide/Girl Scout offices in other countries for information or help with travel plans. It is the policy of the World Association of Girl Guides and Girl Scouts that individual members do not write to national organizations other than their own.

The procedures developed by the World Association help to protect the health, safety, security, and interest of travelers and hosts. A trip abroad is the culmination of one to three years of serious planning by girls and leaders.

Troop #1863 obtained information on procedures, guidelines, and preparation from their council and from GSUSA. They held a troop meeting and decided that they would plan to go to Our Cabaña in two years, preferably in December. So Ms. Gruber and the girls began preparing, from researching the climate in Mexico in December, to carrying out money-earning activities, to becoming travel- and culture-wise. Planning to attend two years in

....

"When we visited the Bahamas in June, 14 Bahamian Girl Guides met us where our cruise ship docked in Nassau. We had written to them before our trip. We laughed and sang together for about an hour before we had to go back on board for the captain's dinner. We taught each other many songs and dances. People standing on the ship decks above as well as the taxicab drivers at the dock clapped as we sang and danced. It was a great experience we won't forget!"

–Heide Ashler, age 14, Apalachee Bend Girl Scout Council, Florida

....

advance gave them plenty of time to prepare. Having the support and advice of their leader, council, and GSUSA made a lot of sense, and helped turn the troop's plan into a dream come true.

Here are some suggestions to help prepare for international events:

1. On a map, pinpoint the WAGGGS member countries, Girl Scout national centers, and world centers.

2. Plan a people awareness day. Invite people from different ethnic, religious, and cultural backgrounds to share their heritage and culture.

3. Listen to music from other countries or see a foreign film.

4. Cook international dishes.

5. Learn a foreign language.

6. Conduct global issues workshops with other members of your troop or group. Learn about world hunger, freedom struggles, environmental abuse, and other subjects.

7. Design a board game (or other kind of game) about American history and government.

PLANNING YOUR OWN WIDER OPPORTUNITY

You, too, can sponsor a wider opportunity. Think of the enjoyment you and your troop would get from planning and inviting other Girl Scouts and non-Girl Scouts to a special wider opportunity.

Before starting to plan a wider opportunity, become familiar with the

key elements for designing one. Wider opportunities should be designed to reflect the values that Girl Scouting can offer. They should:

• Meet the needs of girls.

• Follow the basic principles of Girl Scouting.

• Relate to issues of today's world.

• Contribute to community development.

• Develop a sense of belonging to a worldwide movement: the World Association of Girl Guides and Girl Scouts.

• Inspire girls to continue their involvement in the movement.

• Provide girls with opportunities for planning and decision-making.

• Provide girls with opportunities for meeting new people, seeing new places, trying new activities, and working with adults.

Planning the Opportunity—Step by Step

Planning an event could be called the challenge of "how to think of everything." However, you can make your path more manageable by dividing it into steps, each of which can stand on its own.

STEP 1:
DECIDE ON THE WIDER OPPORTUNITY YOU WOULD LIKE TO DO

Once you and your group decide that you want to hold a wider opportunity, make a list of about six possible activities or events you might want to do. Then select two or three choices. For each of the choices, consider:

1. Its purpose.

2. Its potential benefits.

3. The need for this kind of opportunity in your troop or group, neighborhood, or community.

4. The key elements of a Girl Scout wider opportunity.

5. The number of participants and whom to invite. The date, time, and length of the opportunity.

6. Whether this is the right time of year to have this particular kind of activity.

7. Other activities that may be going on at the same time as yours.

8. Personal, school, household, and other obligations that could possibly restrict your group from holding the event.

9. Health and safety factors and necessary permissions from your Girl Scout council, community organizations, etc.

10. The cost. (Think of costs for food, location rental, transportation, equipment, supplies, etc.)

11. Who will become project officers (director, assistant director, secretary, treasurer) and what their responsibilities will be.

12. Who will serve as adult consultants and what other resources are needed.

After weighing the strengths and weaknesses of the two or three activities or events that you have selected, take a vote to decide which one is best to do.

STEP 2:
DEFINE THE OPPORTUNITY

Discuss, plan, and list the following:
• Purpose of the event.

• Desired results (what you want participants to get out of it).

• Agenda or itinerary.

• Dates and times (include several as backup).

• Participants (the number of people expected to attend, whom to invite).

• Qualifications or requirements for participation.

• Name, theme, or focus.

• Project officers.

• Names, addresses, and telephone numbers of individuals who will serve as contact people.

STEP 3:
IDENTIFY YOUR NEEDS AND RESOURCES

Make a list of everything you will need to complete your activity. Think of what you will need before, during, and after the event.

The list may include advice, supplies, equipment, activity ideas, location/site, books, training, transportation, people, food, publicity, work space, budget, etc.

Resource people are very valuable. They can help decrease the cost of the project, evenly divide or decrease the workload, enrich the content, and increase visibility and recognition. They can help the event run smoothly.

Your wider opportunity needs and resource list might look something like the one used for the "Sports Day for Daisy and Brownie Girl Scouts" on page 37.

STEP 4:
LIST AREAS OF RESPONSIBILITY: WHO WILL DO WHAT?

So that everybody contributes to the success of the project, the responsibility for seeing it through should be shared by each girl in your troop or group. By forming planning teams, each girl can select an area of responsibility in which to work.

You might have planning teams for: acquiring the site for the event,

Wider opportunities can be challenging and fun. They can place you in the center of a series of widening circles, whirling you from the inner circles of your dreams to the outer circles of the world. Wider opportunities can be the start of something big for you!

planning the program, arranging transportation, and providing refreshments. What other planning teams can you think of? Depending on how large your troop or group is, a planning team may consist of two to four girls. Each girl should volunteer to serve on a planning team, since that is where the work of putting on an event takes place.

STEP 5:
DEVELOP A WORK SCHEDULE

Each planning team should develop a realistic plan for beginning and completing the things that it needs to do. (See the sample work schedule.) Put your list in order of priorities. Ask your leader to assist you.

STEP 6:
ALL SET AND READY TO GO! CARRY OUT THE WIDER OPPORTUNITY

When hosting a wider opportunity, begin by welcoming participants, staff, and resource people with a smile. Be pleasant and helpful. Have a good time!

All workers should be at their assigned areas in advance and ready to go. Check with project officers and other team members periodically for any last-minute instructions or changes.

Make sure someone is assigned to take photographs, videos, or notes so you'll have a record of the day for evaluation and publicity purposes.

STEP 7:
FOLLOW UP AND EVALUATE

When the wider opportunity is over, make sure to return or replace materials, distribute thank-you notes and letters, and evaluate the event. You may want to skip the evaluation step, but don't. The evaluation process will provide information that can improve your next event. When you evaluate, ask yourself:

1. How smoothly did the event go? Were there aspects that did not go well?

2. What would you do differently next time?

This is a section of a sample work schedule a Cadette troop might develop for Sports Day. It includes the name of the Cadette Girl Scout who has the responsibility as well as the names of the Brownie Girl Scouts she is working with. Note that the names of the Brownies are three of the characters in the "Here Come the Brownies" series published by Grosset and Dunlap.

Cadette	Brownie	Job	Step #1	Step #2	Step #3
CANDY	Corrie Amy Jo Ann	Promotion and Publicity	Make signs and posters to promote Sports Day.	Ask local stores and businesses to display posters.	Talk to Corrie's mom about placing a Sports Day advertisement in the newspaper.

SPORTS DAY FOR DAISY AND BROWNIE GIRL SCOUTS

This is a "Needs" and "Resource" list a Cadette troop or group might devise for a "Sports Day" event.

NEEDS	RESOURCES
1. Project description	Your troop or group leader.
2. Advice on holding a Girl Scout wider opportunity	Leader, council, *Safety-Wise*, this *Cadette Girl Scout Handbook*, *The Guide for Cadette and Senior Girl Scout Leaders*, other girls who have held wider opportunities.
3. Program activities	*Brownie Girl Scout Handbook*, *The Guide for Daisy Girl Scout Leaders*, *The Guide* for *Brownie Girl Scout Leaders*, films, videos, books, ideas from Daisy and Brownie Girl Scouts, friends, family, teachers, leaders, librarians, and sports groups.
4. Equipment and supplies	Physical education teachers, coaches, community sports and recreation groups, local council.
5. People to help conduct Sports Day	Friends in and out of Girl Scouting: coaches, teachers, family, and community sports and recreation people who can serve as guest speakers, demonstrators, helpers, etc.
6. Location/site	School, council, community center, local park service.
7. Health, safety, and security regulations	*Safety-Wise*, leader, council, sports and recreation staff, physical education teacher, coach, location/site director, school nurse, first-aid instructors, and government officials.
8. Promotion and publicity	Local radio stations, newspapers, stores, schools, local colleges and universities, public library, leader, council media people.
9. Work space	Home; parent's place of work; community, civic, or religious center; public library; Girl Scout council; local museum; meeting room.
10. Refreshments	Family, friends, neighbors, community organizations, local stores.
11. Transportation	Family, friends, leader, council, public transportation.
12. Budget	Leader, family, neighbors, accounting students.

LEADERSHIP AND TROOP OR GROUP GOVERNMENT

WHO IS A LEADER?

Leaders are people who inspire others to bring about change or to get something accomplished. Leadership isn't confined to elected officers. At different times and in a variety of situations, everybody has the opportunity to be a leader. Leaders possess a variety of talents, skills, and traits that are not the same for each leader. Everybody has leadership potential in one situation or another.

Leadership often depends on several things—what must be done, the situation, and what people expect. Each of us, at one time or another, is likely to be in the position of leading a group.

Leaders often take on various roles. The roles they assume may change with time and circumstances and the people with whom they work. Some of these roles are:

Director	Mediator
Problem-solver	Motivator
Facilitator	Guide
Confronter	Producer
Initiator	Timekeeper
Coach	Networker
Clarifier	Peacekeeper
Manager	Explorer
Listener	Nurturer
Delegator	Dreamer

Leadership skills can be learned and practiced in Girl Scouting. You will be able to explore your own ideas about leadership, and develop your abilities.

CADETTE GIRL SCOUTS IN PARTNERSHIP WITH ADULTS

Your adult leader is your resource in the leadership and management of

----

▲ ACTIVITY:

As a leadership skill-building activity, practice as many of the leadership roles listed at the left as possible. For example, when you are in a group, practice being a "listener," a "motivator," or a "networker." Write an entry in your journal about each leadership role you practiced.

----

your group. Adult leadership roles can change according to the group's wishes, needs, and experiences. How much direct leadership the adult takes will depend on how much leadership you and the other girls in your troop or group are willing and able to take.

Adult leaders help you achieve your goals. They are there to listen, support, suggest, guide, and act as resources as you create your own opportunities and activities.

▲ TO CONSIDER:

Identify some situations where you have used your leadership abilities.

CADETTE GIRL SCOUT LEADERSHIP OPPORTUNITIES

Girl Planning Boards

Many councils have planning boards composed of Cadette and/or Senior Girl Scouts. This is an opportunity for Cadette Girl Scouts to meet and work with other girls on councilwide activities. The boards are run by the girls with an adult adviser, and usually meet monthly. In some councils, the board is made up of girls who represent troops, groups, activity centers, and individuals from different geographical areas.

Cadette Girl Scout Program Aide

If you are interested in working directly with a troop, group, or camp unit of younger Girl Scouts, you may volunteer to become a Cadette Girl Scout program aide. As a program aide,

ASTRONAUT

Career Focus

What would I do?
You would conduct experiments in space and gather information about the effect of space on yourself, animals, plants, and/or minerals. You would also deploy, retrieve, and repair satellites.

Where would I work?
During a mission, you would work inside or outside the spacecraft. When you were not on a flight, you would be in training for your next one. This would include physical training as well as increasing your knowledge of everything on the flight, from the engines and computers to your space suit.

What skills and education/training would I need?
You would need to be a risk taker, a clear and logical thinker, and methodical and observant. At minimum, you need a college degree in engineering, physics, biology, or mathematics. There are some physical requirements as well. You also have to have your jet pilot's license and have logged many hours of flying time in high-performance jets. Most astronauts get their education and experience through the U.S. Armed Forces.

Interest Patch Link: Space Exploration.

you will have the opportunity to work directly with younger girls. An adult volunteer or staff member will supervise you as you share your experience and develop your leadership skill.

To become a Cadette Girl Scout program aide you must have completed the sixth grade. Your leader or council representative can provide you with more information about this opportunity. You will receive approximately 10 hours of training and then you will give 25 hours of service. Through instruction from your council, you will specialize in an area such as science, crafts, or adapting activities for girls with disabilities, and then put your skills to work in troops, day camps, or special council events. See page 131 for information about program aide recognitions.

Becoming a Cadette Girl Scout program aide will not only provide you with a unique leadership opportunity but it will prepare you to become a Leader-in-Training or Counselor-in-Training when you are a Senior Girl Scout.

Delegate to the National Council of Girl Scouts of the United States of America

As a Girl Scout 14 years or older, you are eligible to be a delegate to the National Council, which meets every three years. Delegates, who are elected by their council, serve for three years; they voice their opinions and vote on issues critical to the future of Girl Scouting.

Your Cadette Girl Scout years can be as full and as rich with opportunities as you are willing to make them. Take advantage of the variety of experiences available to you.

GROUP COMMUNICATION

Brainstorming

Brainstorming is a special kind of communication for collecting a lot of ideas in a short time. The key is imagination, not practicality or logic, with everyone expressing whatever ideas come to mind. When brainstorming:

• All ideas are welcome without criticism—that comes later.

• The more inventive the idea, the better.

• Quantity of ideas is what is needed; quality can come later.

Building on others' ideas is welcome in

brainstorming. Select a group recorder, someone who can write quickly to keep up with the rush of ideas. Or use a tape recorder. Select someone to start and stop the discussion and agree on a signal to use whenever someone makes a judgmental comment such as "That won't work" or "That's silly."

Write the brainstorming subject on a chalkboard or paper that all can see, and you're ready to go. When the recorder has collected many ideas, stop and take a look at what you have.

When you start judging ideas instead of merely collecting them, brainstorming ends. At that time, you should categorize your ideas as follows: ideas your group can use, ideas that do not seem as if they will work, and ideas that might turn into something useful if developed.

Discussion

Group discussion is talking with a purpose. It can help you when you want to exchange ideas, thoughts, and feelings; increase your knowledge about a particular subject; make a decision; or solve a problem. Getting the most out of discussions and using discussion as a step to action take skill and practice on everyone's part.

Here are some guidelines for leading a discussion:

• See that everyone is comfortable. Seat people in such a way that no one feels left out and everyone can see and hear.

• Start by stating the purpose of the discussion simply and clearly.

• At first—listen. Let others talk so you can find out if they fully understand the purpose of the discussion.

• Make sure every speaker gets respectful attention.

• In cases where things get noisy and confused, raise your hand for quiet if you are working with other Girl Scouts. Lowering your own voice to a whisper may get everyone's attention, too.

• Be prepared with correct information when it is needed, or have a resource nearby with the facts.

• In small groups, try to get the discussion going back and forth among various members rather than from each member to you. In large or more formal groups, all discussion should go through the leader or moderator.

• Summarize the discussion. Repeat the main points that have been made or arguments pro and con and bring the discussion to an end.

Voting and Consensus

Voting and consensus are two ways to close the discussion with a decision. Voting can be done by secret ballot, raising hands, standing up, voice, or ballot box. Each vote should be recorded if the outcome is to be pooled with others: for example, count each vote if all patrol votes are to be added together to get a single troop vote.

To decide by consensus, the entire group considers alternatives and comes to a decision that all members can

Rigoberta Menchú, a Guatemalan Indian woman, is an example of a leader in the area of human rights. In 1992, she was awarded the Nobel Peace Prize in recognition of her achievements toward gaining rights for Indians. Menchú's autobiography, I, Rigoberta Menchú: An Indian Woman in Guatemala, describes the culture and life of a Guatemalan Indian village.

support. By considering all points of view, and, perhaps, by weaving together the best of the alternatives, the group reaches a consensus, an opinion agreed to by all participants.

TROOP GOVERNMENT

Patrols

The patrol system is a representative form of government in which the troop breaks into small groups called patrols. Because your troop or group is divided into smaller units, every patrol member can have a say and a chance to try out leadership roles. Each patrol has a leader, elected by the members, who has the following responsibilities:

• To conduct regular patrol meetings.

• To lead discussions and offer suggestions.

• To take charge of special assignments.

• To delegate responsibilities to patrol members.

• To help her patrol organize to get the work done.

• To consult with adult leaders/partners.

• To represent the patrol at Court of Honor meetings.

The Court of Honor consists of the adult leader, all patrol leaders, plus a troop treasurer and secretary elected from the total group. At Court of Honor meetings, the patrol leaders voice the ideas and opinions of their patrols, and make decisions and plans that will affect the total group.

Executive Board

An executive board (also known as a steering committee) is a small group within the total group, and is made up of officers (president, vice-president, secretary, treasurer, etc.) elected by everyone. This system can be effective for a large group that wishes to have a small, elected representative group serve as the leadership team for everyone.

The executive board gathers ideas from all members, sorts through them, and recommends some of the activities. It plans and coordinates activities and events for the total group, and involves all members in carrying out plans.

The executive board frequently has discussions with the total group and acts as the group's liaison with outside groups. An adult leader acts as adviser to the executive board.

Town Meeting

In the town meeting system, every member of the group discusses and decides on group business. This system is usually most effective in groups of less than 20. Moderators may be selected by the total group to guide discussions and help the group arrive at decisions, or members may just take turns carrying out these responsibilities.

Sometimes, task groups or committees are formed to pursue interests or activities that cannot be handled or enjoyed by the total group.

PLANNING FOR THE YEAR

It is important to plan what your troop or group will be doing for the coming year so everyone knows exactly what's ahead.

To get the big picture, use a calendar to identify activities that will take place during each month. A long-range calendar (see the sample) is helpful when you need to accommodate a number of different activities into a total group action plan. Place a "T" next to the activities to be done by the total group. Place an "S" next to the activities that will be done by a subgroup.

The sample calendar is for a group that has many interests.

Sample Long-Range Calendar

SEPTEMBER
Planning meetings	(T)
Money-earning event	(T)
Apply for wider opportunities	(S)

OCTOBER
Camping trip	(T)
Cycling interest project	(S)
Photography interest project	(S)

NOVEMBER
Community service project	(T)
Photo exhibit of bicycle trips to combine interest project group efforts	(S)
Cycling interest project (continued)	
Photography interest project (continued)	

DECEMBER
Holiday party (international dinner)	(T)
Complete interest projects	(S)

JANUARY
Career Exploration interest project	(S)
Cadette Girl Scout Challenge	(S)
Auto Maintenance interest project	(S)

FEBRUARY
Planning and evaluation	(T)
Career Exploration interest project (continued)	
Cadette Girl Scout Challenge (continued)	
Auto Maintenance interest project (continued)	

MARCH
Council cookie sale	(T)
Fashion and beauty workshop	(T)
Service project planning	(S)
Complete interest projects	(S)

(T)-*activities to be done by the total group.*

(S)-*activities that will be done by a subgroup.*

BUDGETING

Some of what your group does and the plans you make will depend on money. Recording and projecting your needs and the cash required to meet those needs is basically what a budget is all about.

Here is a sample worksheet that you can follow to help plan a yearly budget. First, figure out your proposed outgo—how much you plan to spend. Here are some expenses you might consider:

PROPOSED OUTGO

Girl Scout Annual Membership dues
(National dues multiplied by number of girls in the group.) $_____

Meeting Equipment
(Do you need things like a new bulletin board or supplies for the first-aid kit?) $_____

Resources
(Books, magazines, videos, or other materials that support your troop's or group's work.) $_____

Continuing Program
(Will you need money for service projects, activities with other Girl Scouts, or other long-term plans?) $_____

Flexible Program
(Money for spur-of-the-moment ideas.) $_____

Special Events
(Can include camping, trips, and councilwide events.) $_____

TOTAL PROPOSED OUTGO $_____

To figure out how much money the outgo will "cost" each girl, divide the total proposed outgo by the number of girls in the troop or group. Next, figure out a plan to get the group income to match the proposed outgo.

EXPECTED INCOME

Troop/Group Dues $_____

Product Sales Revenue $_____

Troop Money-Earning Projects $_____

TOTAL EXPECTED INCOME $_____

Life is like a blank sheet of music,
You write the song,
Slow, fast, loud, soft, sweet, sad,
Sometimes realizing a mistake too late,
Sometimes struggling to find the right notes,
But always ending up a masterpiece.

–Meghan Gagliardi, age 14,
Girl Scouts—
Illinois Crossroads
Council, Illinois

SELF-ESTEEM AND HEALTHY LIVING

Chapter 3

WHAT IS SELF-ESTEEM?

ESTEEM: *To set a value, whether high or low, to estimate, to value.*

The definition above describes an important concept in the lives of adolescent girls. Self-esteem is how much you value your worth as a person. Have you ever failed a test and thought "I'm a loser" or flipped through a fashion magazine and thought "I'm so ugly" or made an error while playing a sport and groaned "I'm a real klutz"? These are all examples of experiencing low self-esteem. You are feeling low self-esteem when you are concentrating on aspects of your personality, aptitude, or appearance that you do not perceive as favorable.

On the other hand, when you got an A on a paper, you may have thought "I'm a really talented writer." Maybe you trained conscientiously for a race, ran your best time ever, and thought "I'm a pretty good runner." Feeling good about yourself and your skills is a measure of positive self-esteem.

Self-esteem is not a fixed feeling. In fact, your perceptions of self-worth can vary from day to day and situation to situation.

▲ ACTIVITY:

Answer the following questions in a journal or on this page.

1. What are two accomplishments you feel proud about?

....

....

2. What two things do you do well?

....

....

3. What three qualities do you most like about yourself?

....

....

4. What makes you happier than anything else?

....

....

RECOGNIZING YOUR STRENGTHS

Recognizing and developing your abilities—in sports, in school, in music—will enhance your self-esteem, and there's a lot to be said about that.

But your abilities alone do not define your value as an individual. *You* define your value as an individual. What you think about yourself influences what you do and affects how others respond to you.

▲ ACTIVITY:

Many times other people recognize your strengths better than you do. This activity will help you discover which strengths others recognize in you.

At the top of a sheet of 8 1/2" x 11" paper, write the title "My Strengths." Fold the paper lengthwise into three equal columns. Then divide the paper in half by drawing a horizontal line through the middle. This will give you six equal boxes. Label each box as shown. In the "Me" box, write three of your strengths. Now interview five people who fit in the categories of the remaining boxes. Ask each to name three strengths they believe you have. Write their responses in the appropriate boxes. At your next troop or group meeting, or with a friend or relative, discuss these questions:

My Strengths		
Me	Family Member	Neighbor
Male Friend	Female Friend	Teacher

1. How do you feel about the strengths people recognize in you?

2. Did anybody identify a strength you didn't know you had?

3. Is there a strength you recognize in yourself that nobody else recognized? If so, how can you make people aware of it?

4. Did more than one person identify the same or similar strengths?

WHO AM I?

Who am I really?

What do I want to be?

When I look into the mirror,

Oh, is that really me?

Why do I say such foolish things?

Things I never mean.

One moment real, the next an image,

Things just aren't what they seem.

Why can't I show them who I am?

Is it fear, or maybe pride?

Where is a friend who is willing to listen?

In whom can I confide?

Doesn't anyone understand

What it's like to hide your feelings away?

To keep them bundled up inside,

To save for when I pray?

I search to find who that is,

The stranger deep inside of me.

Who am I really?

Will anyone ever see?

—Molly Bennett, age 15,
Mid-Continent Girl Scout Council,
Missouri

SELF-ACCEPTANCE: WHY IS IT SO HARD?

At this time in your life, being different is probably the last thing you want to be. But being different is exactly what you have in common with everybody else. You may grow up so fast and tall that you tower over all your friends. Your body may mature very early, or you may be a "late bloomer" and not mature until way after your friends. You may have some difficulty reading or walking or hearing. Being teased or ridiculed by others for being different can really hurt your self-esteem. On the other hand, if you find the need to tease or hurt others, you should examine your motives. Often, people who intentionally hurt others have low self-esteem and insecurities of their own.

Do you think that the "beautiful" or "brilliant" girls are so fortunate, that everything comes their way? If you are perceptive enough, you will find that neither beauty nor brain power guarantees a positive body image or high self-esteem.

BODY IMAGE AND SELF-ESTEEM

For girls more so than boys, body image and self-esteem are strongly linked. When girls dislike their bodies, they often have difficulty liking themselves. Some girls are overly concerned about physical attractiveness; in fact, many girls go on their first diet by the time they're eight or nine years old!

By the time you reached school age, you had received countless messages from a variety of sources—newspapers, magazines, television, movies, family, friends, school—about what is considered beautiful and what you must do to attain it (or at least come close to it). This "standard of beauty" is an unattainable ideal for most people, yet many girls and women spend a lifetime in the often unhappy, expensive search. It causes some women to become artificial imitations of somebody else's ideal.

How do you prevent yourself from getting caught up in the chase for the elusive and often unattainable "standard of beauty"? First of all, take a look at all of the people and institutions who would benefit from your attempt to look like somebody you're not: cosmetics companies, the fashion industry, advertising companies, plastic surgeons, the diet industry. Those companies have a stake in your attempt to look like the "ideal" beauty. Some of them, such as cosmetics companies and the fashion industry, can also help you enhance your own natural looks. The difference is in your own attitude. If you decide not to invest in fantasy but to aim at looking your best, you can discover or create a style of your own.

My eyes are chilled, my nose is cold,
My hair's unkempt the while;
My skirt is short, my knees are blue
I'm stiff but I'm in style

–Amanda Darlak, age 17,

Girl Scout Council of the Nation's Capital, District of Columbia

People with high self-esteem tend to:

Be tolerant of themselves and others.

Have a belief in their own abilities.

Make realistic judgments about themselves.

Be less prone to depression.

Have self-confidence.

Be assertive.

For Self-Reflection—A Body Image Quiz

PERFECTION

Perfection isn't a miracle.
Perfection is like a disease.
Don't get the perfection infection,
It's worse than having the fleas!

—Janine Rinker, age 14,

Chipeta Girl Scout Council, Colorado

The quiz below will help you recognize how you feel about your body and what influences those feelings.

	Yes	No	Comments
1. Does your mood reflect how you think you look that day?	—	—	
2. Do you often take time to plan what you will wear and to coordinate your wardrobe before getting dressed?	—	—	
3. Do you make negative comments about your body or the way you look?	—	—	
4. Is it difficult for you to accept compliments about your appearance?	—	—	
5. Can you think of occasions where you felt really good about how you looked? Where you felt not so good?	—	—	
6. Are you self-conscious about some part of your body? Which parts?	—	—	
7. Do you worry about your weight?	—	—	
8. If asked to describe yourself, do the positives outnumber the negatives?	—	—	

Your self-concept includes much more than your physical appearance. Your identity as a family member, Girl Scout, student, community volunteer, friend, sister, etc., your skills, abilities, sense of humor, plans, goals, and interests all make a statement about who you are.

TAKING CARE OF YOUR APPEARANCE

Your choice of clothes, hairstyle, and perhaps makeup can be a means of expressing your personality and tastes.

Clothes

Having suitable clothes for all the occasions and activities in your life isn't easy, especially when money is limited. Remember, when buying clothes, to consider that you are growing fast, that

certain colors will suit you best, and that how you spend your time should influence your purchase decisions.

Decide how to get the most from the clothes you already have. For example, put outfits together in different combinations. Next, decide what to buy to round out your wardrobe.

When shopping for clothes, ask yourself:

- Is this for *me*? Is it becoming to my face and figure?
- Will I get good use from it?
- Is the price within my budget?

▲ ACTIVITY:

Host a fashion show around a theme. Have girls in your troop or group model.

- Will it go with things I already own?
- Does it fit properly?
- Is it machine washable or does it need to be dry cleaned?
- Does it seem likely to wrinkle or fade?
- Is the style right for my age and usual activities?
- Will I still like it a month from now?
- Can it be worn for more than one season of the year?

"...Being Barbie for a day might have some frilly advantages, but I'll take my chances and follow the courage of Joan of Arc...."

–Sandra Taninies, age 17,

Moingona Girl Scout Council, Iowa

Makeup

The decision to wear makeup is a personal one. Many people choose not to use any makeup; others may use just lipstick or eye makeup. Makeup can enhance your attractiveness and highlight your best features. Using it depends on when you are ready and when your parents or guardians give you permission to use it.

Here are some tips on using makeup:

• Cleanse your face before applying makeup.

• Use shades that match your natural skin tones.

• Avoid using too much makeup.

• Ask others' opinions about what looks best on you.

• Be careful not to apply eye makeup too close to the inside of your eye.

• Never share makeup, especially eye makeup, with others. Bacteria can spread easily.

• Never go to bed without taking off your makeup. Use a cleanser that is right for your skin type.

Looking good for yourself is more important than trying to look like or please someone else. Be happy with the special person you see each day in the mirror.

▲ ACTIVITIES:

1. With your troop or group, plan and conduct a beauty workshop. Invite consultants to discuss health and fitness. Ask them to demonstrate makeup application and proper care of skin, hair, and teeth.

2. Make your own cleansing facial. Mix one tablespoon of raw bran (available in supermarkets and health-food stores) with two tablespoons of plain yogurt and one teaspoon of wheat germ or vegetable oil. Mix to form a thick paste. Apply the mixture with your fingertips, using gentle, circular motions. The bran helps shed dead skin cells, the oil lubricates, and the yogurt cleanses, cools, and tightens.

SELF-ESTEEM AND CULTURAL IDENTITY

Concepts of beauty are culturally determined. Chinese women were once forced to conform to their culture's ideal that women should have small feet. Young girls had their feet bound by age eight. In some African societies, scarification—the process of scarring the face with a sharp instrument to create elaborate designs—is a sign of beauty. In the United States, many girls pierce their ears and other body parts.

As a member of a particular ethnic group, you possess specific characteristics that you inherited. Some of these characteristics, such as the shape of your eyes, the size of your nose, your skin coloring, even your height, may reflect your ethnic heritage. It would be unfair for anyone to require you to conform to one standard of beauty when beauty comes in so many forms. Accepting yourself and your natural beauty is an important step in being happy and healthy.

Everybody belongs to a cultural or ethnic group, and it is healthy to have pride in your heritage. Learning about your heritage will contribute to your positive sense of self. Feelings of pride come from studying your cultural group's history, literature, and culture. Next in importance is interacting with people who are different from you, and learning about their cultural or racial heritages. In that way, you will learn to value the differences all people bring to our society, and to respect these differences without placing a value on them. (See "Achieving Pluralism Through the Four Program Goals," page 12, for more about pluralistic values.)

Extending a sense of belonging and self-worth to all girls is a goal of Girl Scouting. You along with all Girl Scouts are encouraged to see the value of people different from you.

▲ ACTIVITIES:

Do one of the following activities with Girl Scouts of an ethnic or cultural background different than yours.

1. Conduct a cross-cultural survey of past customs and fashions. Ask older women and men from your family and from different ethnic groups about the customs and fads they witnessed and/or participated in when they were growing up.

2. Many movie stars, recording artists, and other well-known people have tried not to look like a mass-produced image. Instead, they have projected their own unique style. Identify some people you know, famous or not, who fit this category. Collect pictures of them to make a montage.

3. From different media sources, select advertisements using women and children to sell products. Discuss the images of women and children, and how they are used to sell the products. The Contemporary Issues book, *Developing Health and Fitness: Be Your Best!* contains additional activities on this topic.

GENDER BIAS

Adolescent girls often have lower self-esteem than adolescent boys. This is believed to be a result of the pressures society places on girls to be quiet and kind, to please others, and to conform to the accepted standards of feminine appearance and behavior. Have you ever heard someone say: "Be quiet; act like a lady," or "Girls aren't good at science"? These kinds of remarks are "gender biased." That means these remarks are based on stereotypes about girls and women. (For more on stereotypes, see page 59.) A person who makes these kinds of remarks is not looking at women and girls as individuals, but is unfairly deciding what all females can and cannot do or be simply because they are female.

You can respond to gender-biased comments by saying, "Not all girls are alike. We all have different interests and abilities." When people are asked to explain their remarks, they sometimes realize how hurtful or silly they sound. If someone says something that hurts you, tell them the effect it had on you. You have no control over their feelings and attitudes, but you can let them know how you were affected by what they said or did.

▲ TO CONSIDER:

One university study reports that in families where both parents work full-time, teenage girls do ten hours of housework a week. That's three times more than their brothers do.

GENDER BIAS IN SCHOOL

Angie Speaks to Her Math Teacher

Angie's math teacher, Ms. Hope, always calls on the boys in the class first. Angie decides to tell Ms. Hope how she feels.

• "Ms. Hope, I need to talk to you about something that is really bothering me. Today in class I noticed that you always call on the boys first to answer the problems.

• This really upsets me, because I worked hard to do the problems last night. You didn't give any of us girls a chance to give the first answer to a question.

• Would it be possible for you to alternate between boys and girls when you ask for the answers?

• I am going to continue to raise my hand in class when I know the answer, so that you can call on me and the other girls in class in the future."

▲ ACTIVITIES:

1. Turn the "Angie Speaks to her Math Teacher" scenario into a role-playing situation. Create a part for Ms. Hope by anticipating how the dialogue might go with her in it. Then act out the drama.

2. The following role-playing scenarios give you some more opportunities to practice assertive behavior with friends. (For information on "speaking up for yourself," see pages 91–92.)

- Someone cuts in front of you in a concert line.
- A friend borrowed ten dollars and hasn't paid it back.
- Some man who says he's your dad's friend offers you a ride home from school.
- You're at a party when a popular boy offers you a cigarette.

Researchers who study the way students and teachers interact in school have discovered that girls are often treated differently than boys by both male and female teachers (Angie's situation in math class is all too common). In many classrooms, boys get more of the teacher's attention than girls, and they are commended more on their ideas. Sometimes this is because boys misbehave more in school. Receiving more of the teacher's attention—even in a negative way—can give students an edge in school.

In some school districts, girls have requested all-girl classes to help eliminate this form of bias. It's important to note that not only males are guilty of gender bias. Females have also exhibited gender bias in school and in social settings.

GENDER BIAS IN SPORTS

Some schools practice bias against girls in sports and other extracurricular activities. But there are laws to protect girls from this form of bias. Title IX, for instance, requires school districts to provide equal opportunities to girls in athletic programs. If you have been denied a place on a school team by a coach or teacher because of your gender, speak to your parent or guardian and school authorities.

▲ FOR DISCUSSION:

Identify the types of gender bias you or your friends have experienced. How did you respond? How would you respond now?

YOUR VALUES

Values are what you believe in and what is important to you. Your values are shaped and influenced by your family, friends, school, religion, media, the country in which you live, your Girl Scout experience, and many other things. The more you are aware of your own values, the more your behavior will be consistent with what you truly feel and believe.

At this time in your life, you are facing many challenges. You are continuing your education, developing relationships with peers and family, and dealing with your evolving sexuality. Through all this, your values serve as foundations for your decisions and actions.

....

▲ ACTIVITY:

To help you explore attitudes, values, and interests, complete these sentences. Look for patterns in your responses:

During my free time, I like to _be with friends_

When I'm 25 years old _I be starring in a hit comedy movie_

Some of the things I like best about life are _my humor_

I could help make the world a better place by _donating my time_

I feel sad when _I'm made fun of_

I get angry when _I'm made fun of_

I'm happiest when _I'm in 6/7 p._

My friends are _Brittany, Brina, Michelle, Lisha ect_ very important

My family is _Me Mom Pop Cort_

....

DECIDING WHAT'S IMPORTANT TO YOU

Use the following chart to help you learn about your own values. Put a #1 next to the most important value, a #2 next to the next most important value, etc. Add your own values to the list, too. Look at the list again in six months. What's changed? What have you learned about yourself by doing this exercise?

p. 3.06

VALUES

	How I Feel Now Date:	Six Months Later Date:
Doing well in school	3	
Caring for the environment	12	
Spending time with my family	2	
Being popular	7	
Being helpful	11	
Wearing expensive clothes	10	
Having a boyfriend	8	
Knowing all the latest trends	9	
Volunteering in my community	13	
Excelling in sports	14	
Being happy	4	
Being active politically	16	
Staying healthy	5	
Being with friends	1	
Earning money	6	
Participating in religious activities	15	
Other values:		

Spend at least one week cultivating and appreciating some of the things you selected on your values list. If you wrote that you value your family, spend time with them and let them know how you value them. Do this with as many topics from your list as you wish.

VALUING OTHERS

In this increasingly complex and segmented world, you can become a positive, constructive force. Think about what you can do to work for positive change.

Prejudice

To be prejudiced against a person or group of people is to make judgments about them before getting to know them. Someone can be prejudiced against someone else because of her dress, social status, age, sex, religion, skin color, or disability. Judging a person on the way she dresses, for example, is making a decision about her character, abilities, and talents based on outward appearance. In reality, a person's outside appearance, skin color, or physical condition does not indicate how she feels and thinks on the inside, or what her abilities are.

▲ **TO CONSIDER:**

What are some ways you can actively help end prejudice?

Why are some people prejudiced and others more accepting of people? Often prejudice evolves out of fear. People tend to fear what they don't know. They avoid the hard work of becoming

Career Focus

ASSISTANT DISTRICT ATTORNEY

What would I do?
You would be the prosecuting attorney for the state or nation in a criminal trial. That would entail helping the police gather evidence, researching past trials and laws, and presenting your case to the grand jury. If the defendant is indicted, you would prepare to present your case to the jury and judge.

Where would I work?
Most of the time you would work in the district attorney's offices alongside the other lawyers. Frequently, your work would take you to police precincts and crime scenes. Eventually, you would try your case in a courtroom.

What skills and education/training would I need?
You need to be organized and exact, have good problem-solving skills, and the ability to communicate with and persuade others effectively. A college degree is necessary to get into law school. To become an attorney, you must complete law school and pass your state's bar exam.

Interest Patch Link:
The Law.

▲ FOR DISCUSSION:

Have you ever been the victim of prejudice? Have you ever been guilty of prejudiced thinking? Share your experiences and thoughts on this topic with the other girls in your troop or group.

acquainted with those who have different backgrounds. Prejudiced thinking may be learned in our society from the media, interaction with others, schools and textbooks, even from parents and neighbors. People who are prejudiced are more likely to have feelings of low self-worth than those who aren't.

Do your part to stop the spread of prejudice. One way is to refuse to be even a silent participant by listening to ethnic jokes. You could speak out against them. This might encourage others who feel the same way to speak up also.

▲ FOR DISCUSSION:

Have you or anyone you know ever been discriminated against? Share these experiences. Work on a community service project that addresses prejudice and discrimination.

Stereotyping

A stereotype is a general belief, usually negative, about all members of a particular group of people. The general belief grows out of misunderstanding and ignorance. As with prejudice,

▲ ACTIVITY:

Conduct a mock city council meeting. Select a mayor and city council members who will hold a meeting to discuss discrimination and other problems in your city. Prepare an agenda for your meeting.

stereotyping involves prejudging. The stereotype goes something like this:

"Sandy is really skinny and she is very shy. All skinny people are shy."

"That woman hit a tree while she was parking her car. All women are bad drivers."

Discrimination

To discriminate against people is to act negatively toward them because of their race, religion, sex, or other distinction. Discrimination closes the doors of opportunity to jobs, housing, schooling, and friendships. Stereotypes are often used to justify discrimination.

Good Health in Action

Being healthy involves decisions you make for yourself—decisions concerning what to eat, how to be physically active, how much sleep to get, when to see a doctor, what safety measures to follow, how to relate to other people, and how to relax. You make these decisions continuously and as time passes you create a lifestyle for yourself. You can take steps now to ensure that your lifestyle is healthy and satisfying.

BEING AWARE OF PHYSICAL AND EMOTIONAL CHANGES

The passage from childhood to adulthood, including the physical changes that mark puberty, is an important turning point in your life. This transition could last several years. As your body is changing, you may experience abrupt physical growth, mood swings, or feelings of inadequacy. Sexual thoughts and daydreams are common. And, of course, as you

Career Focus

PHYSICAL THERAPIST

What would I do?
You would help people cope with physical pain and disability caused by disease or injury. First you'd test patients to discover the cause or limits of their impediment. Then you'd design programs of treatment and oversee their implementation. These treatments might include massage, heat and cold treatments, exercises, and ultrasound. In addition, you would teach patients how to use equipment such as crutches and wheelchairs.

Where would I work?
You could work in a hospital, nursing home, rehabilitation facility, in your own office, or in patients' homes.

What skills and education/training would I need?
Since physical therapists work closely with doctors and other health professionals, you would need to be comfortable working on a team. Clear communication as well as good observational skills are important, too. A college degree is the minimum requirement. In addition, you need practical experience, which can be obtained through college course work, a certificate program, or a master's degree. Finally, you must pass a state licensing exam.

Interest Patch Link:
Tune In to Well-Being; Sports.

A GUIDE TO DAILY FOOD CHOICES

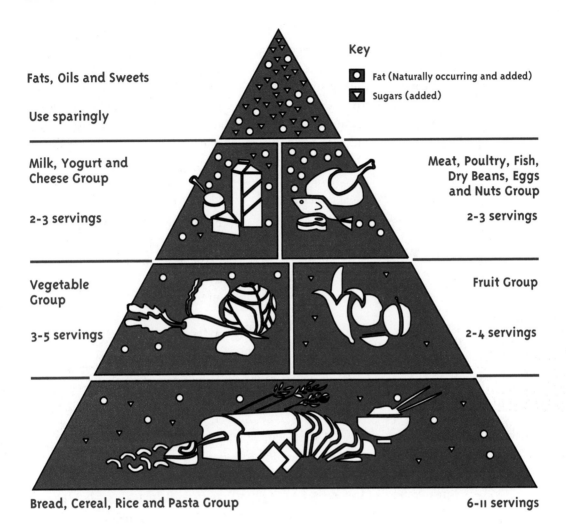

Fats, Oils and Sweets

Use sparingly

Key

◯ Fat (Naturally occurring and added)

▽ Sugars (added)

Milk, Yogurt and Cheese Group

2-3 servings

Meat, Poultry, Fish, Dry Beans, Eggs and Nuts Group

2-3 servings

Vegetable Group

3-5 servings

Fruit Group

2-4 servings

Bread, Cereal, Rice and Pasta Group

6-11 servings

become a young adult, you may desire more independence from adult authority. In many cultures, this is the time when girls assume the responsibilities of adult women.

The physical, emotional, and social changes that occur during your teen years can be confusing. It may be more difficult to find your place in a world that up to now has always been comfortable—school, community, even family. You may find yourself more easily upset or depressed. Talking with someone you trust, recording your feelings in a journal, cultivating a hobby or special interest (see Chapter 6) are some ways of helping you through this emotionally challenging time.

EATING THE RIGHT FOODS

What you eat has an effect on your physical health, appearance, and emotions. Food supplies energy, builds and repairs tissues, and helps regulate bodily processes. The amount of energy that your body gets from the food you eat is measured in calories. Girls from ages 12 to 15 usually need about 2,000 to 2,500 calories a day. These caloric requirements should be supplied by a balanced diet. Carbohydrates, proteins, fats, vitamins, and minerals are the five major nutrients and, along with water, are essential for a healthy body. See the Contemporary Issues booklet *Developing Health and Fitness: Be Your Best!* for more about nutrition.

HEALTH ALERTS

Sex

Too many girls become sexually active for the wrong reasons: they are pressured into it; they think everyone else is doing it; they don't want to lose their boyfriends. Sexual activity has its own set of responsibilities and emotional turmoil. Besides a feeling of deprivation that can result from doing something you weren't ready to do, the consequences of teenage sexual activity may include becoming pregnant, contracting a sexually transmitted disease, and feeling lowered self-esteem and guilt for going against personal values and religious beliefs.

Sexually Transmitted Diseases (STDs)

Each year, one quarter of all sexually active women between the ages of 15 and 19 are treated for an STD.

Some STDs such as genital herpes and genital warts are viruses with no

known cure. They can be treated but not eliminated. Others can be cured with penicillin. Some of the most serious STDs are syphilis and gonorrhea. These and even some of the less serious sexually transmitted infections can affect your ability to become pregnant in the future. Syphilis can damage your brain and lead to blindness if not treated.

Note: The symptoms of some STDs are not always apparent. Therefore, it is extremely important to get treated by a doctor if you suspect you could have an STD.

AIDS

No matter where you live or how protected your life is, you almost certainly have some knowledge of the deadly virus that causes AIDS. The following information is presented here because it is extremely important for you to learn the facts about AIDS to make responsible decisions about your health and well-being.

Many young people think that AIDS doesn't happen in their school, in their community, or in their crowd of friends. They think AIDS is something that happens to "other" people, not them. This gives too many teens a false sense of security. Many people who are diagnosed with the HIV virus in their twenties actually acquired it during their teen years. You can't tell who has the HIV virus or full-blown AIDS by what a person looks like or where she or he lives.

Young people can put themselves at risk for getting the AIDS virus.

What is risky behavior? Risky behavior means doing things that can increase one's chances of getting the AIDS virus. The AIDS virus is transmitted:

• By having unprotected sex with an infected person.

• By sharing unsterilized needles or syringes that have been used by an infected person.

• During birth or through breast-feeding if the mother is infected.

• Through open wounds in which the blood of an infected person enters someone else's bloodstream.

Which behavior is not risky?

• Hugging an infected person.

• Using the toilet after an infected person.

• Befriending an infected person.

The only sure way you can avoid the AIDS virus is by not using intravenous drugs and by abstaining from sex.

Tobacco

Most people who smoke cigarettes begin smoking before the eleventh grade. Tobacco and advertising companies know this and try to sell cigarettes to this age group. Unfortunately, females are still the only growing population of smokers.

Does smoking start out as a rite of passage? Do girls begin smoking to feel grown up? Or to be part of a group? Or to rebel against adult authority? Or

because they don't know what else to do with their hands? Whatever the explanation, there is no good reason to start.

Cigarette ads are designed to attract young people. They make it appear that the product improves a person's popularity, sophistication, and sexual attraction. If your self-esteem is low, you might feel you were missing out on a terrific experience by not smoking. What you really would be missing out on is a habit that's difficult to break and that makes your hair, clothing, and breath smell bad. Smoking can also cause you to develop wrinkles on your face at an early age and could increase your risk for cancer, emphysema, and other deadly diseases. Plus, women who smoke while pregnant can harm their unborn baby. If you start to smoke now, you may spend most of your adult life trying to break this habit.

Drugs and Alcohol

Taking illegal drugs and/or drinking alcohol can have a disastrous effect on a young person. At this stage in life, a young person's body and mind are still growing, and she is discovering her place in the world, learning about herself, developing skills, and forming friendships. Drugs and alcohol can take all of that away from a young person's life. She can lose her ability to laugh and have fun with friends, to study and do well in school, to play the piano, to help her little brother with his homework, to go on a camping trip with her sister Girl Scouts. Involvement with alcohol and illegal drugs does just that. It can get in the way of physical growth and can take away a young person's dreams and goals.

Why is substance abuse—excessive use of drugs and alcohol—so harmful? When a person becomes addicted, she

▲ **FOR DISCUSSION:**

Sexism can be found in many advertisements, especially in alcohol and cigarette ads. Why do you think this is the case?

develops a physical and psychological need for the substance. In other words, her body and mind crave the drug. Her energies are directed towards satisfying the addiction. Using the drug is no longer her choice, but her need. She is preoccupied with such thoughts as where she will get the drug, how she'll get the money to purchase it, where she will hide it, and how she will prevent her family from finding out. Thoughts such as: "Isn't Brian cute; I hope he'll ask me out," or "I must see that movie everybody's talking about" are replaced with thoughts about drugs and alcohol.

People who have abused drugs or alcohol may spend years being rehabilitated and participating in some form of therapy. When they reenter normal life, they have to start from scratch. They may slip backwards, get hooked on drugs again, and have to start all over. At best, they take one day at a time and hope that it's enough. If only they had known that before they took that first snort!

If you feel the need to take drugs or alcohol, stop and think about why. Then, discuss your feelings with your parent, guardian, Girl Scout leader, teacher, school counselor, or trusted adult friend. Take responsibility for your health.

BECOME AN ACTIVIST FOR A HEALTHY, LESS STRESSFUL LIFE!

It is your right and natural inheritance to lead a healthy, happy life. But you have to create such a life for yourself. It doesn't automatically fall into your lap.

Today, leading a healthy life has more to do with having balance in your life. Life is not meant to be all play or all work. Life is a healthy mix that you blend for yourself. And this is a good time for you to create a balanced, healthy lifestyle to carry you into adulthood.

Cruel Apology

*What do you say to someone
That you really hurt?
Do you just ignore the fact
Their face was in the dirt?
You know you should apologize
But sorry's such a little word.
It doesn't get the feeling,
And is seldom ever heard.*

*–Amy Bailey, age 13,
Sybaquay Girl Scout Council,
Illinois*

RELATIONSHIPS WITH FAMILY AND FRIENDS

Chapter 4

FAMILIES

Social relationships are an essential aspect of being human. You grow up within a network of relationships—each one unique. Having relationships with others can add excitement, love, and security to life. Some of the reasons we form relationships are to share activities and interests, to be liked, and to feel special. But rela-tionships can also bring frustration, disappointment, jealousy, and conflict.

Communication is one of the most important elements for maintaining good relationships. Later on in this chapter you will explore some ways to have good communication with others.

....

▲ ACTIVITY:

Write down five things you like most about your family. Do this same activity in three months and one year from now. Compare your responses. Are they the same or different?

....

Whatever its form and however you feel about it, your family is a very important part of your life. Family members support you, help you grow, and love you. But they can also be a source of conflict which takes energy and time to resolve.

WHAT IS A FAMILY?

Families have changed over the years. Today's family can be composed of:

• A single parent with one or more children.

• A mother with a full-time job outside the home, a father who stays at home, and a child.

• A grandmother and grandchild.

• A two-career couple with no children.

• A remarried couple, with children of their own as well as children from their earlier marriages. This family is sometimes called a blended family.

• One or more children living with guardians who are not their birth parents.

• A group of relatives (parents, grandparents, aunts, uncles, or cousins) and others all living together. This family is called an extended family.

Each of these families has its own strengths, weaknesses, and challenges.

ROLES AND RELATIONSHIPS

Being a member of a family means that you are also part of a group. You will be part of many different groups through-out your life. Girl Scouts is an example

Building Your Character Up with Down's

The day finally came
When my baby brother would arrive.
The doctor said there were some problems,
But at least he was alive.
My brother had to stay in the hospital
For a total of three weeks.
My mom and dad could hold and feed him,
But through the window, I could only peek.
When my whole family was together at home,
Friends and neighbors came from all over town
To see my baby brother named Brennan,
Who was born with a syndrome called Down's.
My family didn't know much about Down's Syndrome,
So many things were not clear.
We talked to some parents of children with Down's,
And knew that there was no reason to fear.
I know I am a better person
Since I've had a handicapped brother.
I am more sensitive and caring to all people,
And have more understanding toward others.
When it comes to building my character,
Leadership I must show
To treat handicapped people as human beings
Is the message I want my friends to know.
My brother will go to school
And learn just like you and me,
So he can get an education
And be the best that he can be.

–Allison O'Donnell, age 12,
Audubon Girl Scout Council,
Louisiana

67

of another group to which you belong. Groups have rules and values that guide the behavior of their members and contribute to the smooth functioning of the group. Your family role represents a unique relationship between you and other members of your family.

Your roles and responsibilities at home may be determined by your position in the family or your unique skills or goals. For example, as the oldest in your family, you may assume the role of baby-sitter or peacemaker. You probably assume several roles in your

▲ FOR DISCUSSION:

1. Describe your family. How do the members get along with each other?
2. Discuss stories, novels, and movies you have read or seen that deal with family life and relationships. (Consider examples of family life portrayed in multicultural children's books as well.) Talk about family structure, how the family members relate to one another, and problems or issues confronting the family.

Career Focus

GENERAL MANAGER

What would I do?
You would direct a department or team in a company or business organization to accomplish goals and assignments. You would develop, usually with your department or team, a strategy to accomplish your goals. Other responsibilities include delegating work and overseeing your team's progress, and motivating and assisting department members' actions.

Where would I work?
Usually in an office, although that might vary depending on the field. Corporate managers are in office buildings; manufacturing managers might be in factories or labs; retail managers are in stores.

What skills and education/training would I need?
Good problem-solving and communication skills are essential. You need the ability to supervise and motivate others as well as prioritize tasks effectively. A college degree is needed; you also need to be knowledgeable about the field you are entering. Some companies offer management-training programs.

Interest Patch Link:
Leadership.

daily life and are probably good at changing from one to another: You may be the "baby" in the family at home and the head of the debate team at school. You are probably: a friend, student, daughter, and perhaps a music student, athlete, or tutor.

▲ ACTIVITIES:

1. Make a list of the roles you assume in your daily life. Next to each role, jot down the responsibilities that come with that role. For example, as a student you have a responsibility to attend school every day, complete homework assignments, and work to the best of your ability.

2. Compare sibling relationships in three different families. You might look at what it's like to be the youngest and the oldest in a family of four children versus a family with only two siblings. Or you might explore how twins relate to each other.

RELATIONSHIPS WITH GRANDPARENTS AND OTHER SENIOR CITIZENS

Intergenerational relationships provide a link between older persons, who possess a lifetime of knowledge and skills, and younger persons, who possess a fresh outlook on life. Many senior citizens have the health and vitality to contribute much to a friendship with you and other girls your age.

You can begin a cross-generational friendship with older adults by writing to nursing-home residents, visiting them, and inviting them to attend school or Girl Scout functions. You might invite senior citizens to work with you in small groups on a craft or hobby. Or you could help a senior citizen by escorting her or him to a store or the bank.

WHEN FAMILIES CHANGE

Changes in family structure due to separation, divorce, and remarriage are a reality for many young people today. As a result, a child may have to cope with:

• New relationships.

• Having stepparents.

• Absence of a parent.

• Financial difficulties.

• Living in two households.

• Sharing a room and loss of privacy.

• Less attention.

• Anger and sadness.

Here are some ways to cope with stress that can result from such changes.

• Talk to a family member, teacher, Girl Scout leader, religious leader, or other trusted adult about how you are feeling.

• Write about the situation in a journal.

• Confide in a friend who has experienced family divorce or remarriage.

• Express your feelings through art, music, dance, or another creative outlet.

Remember, most of all, that you don't have to shoulder your sadness, anger, or difficulties alone. No one is expected to endure a stressful situation without the help of others.

Career Focus

PSYCHOLOGIST

What would I do?
Psychologists study human behavior. You would administer tests, conduct lab experiments, and study case histories to help explain how and why people act the way they do. You might explore how people learn, discover why people do or do not grow in one stage of development, or help clients resolve personal problems.

Where would I work?
You could work in schools, colleges, clinics, governmental agencies, youth organizations, private industry, or in private practice.

What skills and education/training would I need?
You'd need the ability to be sensitive and analytical, to listen well, and to solve problems creatively. You'd need a college degree followed by at least a master's and often a doctorate. You might also need to become licensed to practice in your state.

Interest Patch Link:
Understanding Yourself and Others; Tune In to Well-Being.

SPENDING TOO MUCH TIME ON THE TELEPHONE CAN LEAD TO FAMILY CONFLICT.

WHEN FAMILY MEMBERS TALK IT OUT, SOLUTIONS HAPPEN. A 20-MINUTE TIME LIMIT ON CALLS, FOR EXAMPLE, CAN HELP DISSOLVE THE PROBLEM.

FAMILY CONFLICT

As with all relationships, all families have conflicts. Here are a few examples of issues/situations that are a common source of conflict between parents and adolescents:

- Keeping your room clean.
- Dressing "neatly."
- Getting home by a certain hour.
- Not talking on the telephone for too long.
- Taking part in family activities and obligations.
- Dating.
- How you spend your time.
- Doing chores.
- Doing homework.
- Listening to music.
- Getting allowance—how much and how it's spent.

What can you add to the conflict list? Which issues have been the cause of disputes in your family? To help resolve a family conflict, see "Conflict Resolution," page 76.

▲ ACTIVITY:

Use some of the conflicts presented here as subjects for short skits or poems. You can make some of them humorous. Perform them before a group.

Can You Offer a Solution?

The following scenarios represent the kinds of conflict that teenagers and parents experience. Offer your viewpoint on how each problem can be handled.

"My parents invade my privacy. They enter my room without knocking, read my diary, and eavesdrop on me while I talk on the phone. I've told them that they're being unfair, but they keep on doing it. I don't feel trusted."

–An Eighth Grader

This teenager has a right to feel that she isn't being trusted. She should discuss why her parents feel that this is necessary. She might ask herself if she has given them any reason to be suspicious. Then she could tell them how she feels. If she initiates open communication with her parents, she may find out why they feel a need to pry.

"My parents don't like my friends. They say they don't come from 'good' families, and that they have a bad influence on me. I don't care what families they come from. They're my good friends. And why would my parents think I could be influenced by bad behavior anyhow?"

–A Ninth Grader

Parents of teens find that their children are growing more and more independent. Their children are trying out new friendships, venturing to new places, and exploring new activities. Parents are anxious about that. This causes some parents to overreact. If your parents react in this way, show them you are responsible (by remembering to call if you'll be late, for example), and that you choose your friends wisely.

Communication

One of the reasons that conflicts arise between parents and adolescents over rules or other family situations is a lack of communication. When people don't communicate, misunderstandings or misinterpretation of behaviors can result. Good communication is essential in every relationship. You probably don't always say what you really mean nor do you always hear what is being said. And this can create communication problems.

"Listen" to the following exchange.

The Lost Earrings

Fourteen-year-old Rina was getting ready to go to her high school dance. She suddenly burst into tears and ran into her mother's bedroom. "I can't find my earrings," she said, sobbing. "What am I going to do?"

Her mother replied, "Don't worry about it, dear, you can wear my earrings."

Rina looked at her mom. Anger colored her face. She turned toward the door, stormed out of the room, and yelled, "You really don't care, do you?" as she slammed the door behind her.

• Why did Rina react so angrily?

• Did Rina's mom really not care?

• Did Rina's mom understand why her daughter became so angry?

• How could Rina and her mother each say things differently to prevent this misunderstanding?

This situation suffers from each person missing the point. Rina's mother felt that replacing the lost earrings with another pair would solve Rina's problem. Rina didn't want a replacement. She wanted to find and wear her own earrings. She directed her anger and frustration at her mother.

▲ ACTIVITY:

Role-play the "Lost Earrings" situation with a different ending.

DEVELOPING YOUR COMMUNICATION SKILLS

One way to avoid misunderstandings is to be clear about how you feel and what you mean to say. By talking and listening attentively and by identifying your own feelings, you can increase your ability to communicate well with others.

Talking and Listening

In describing the behavior that bothers you, here are some ways you can try to be specific.

Use "I" messages instead of "you" messages to help you communicate in a more direct fashion. Here is a simple formula for "I" messages.

When you _____, I feel

_____

_____

because_____

_____

_____.

First describe the behavior that bothers you; then state how it makes you feel. Next, identify the effect it has on you and why. For example: "When you yell at me in front of my friends, I feel embarrassed because they'll think I'm a baby."

Identifying Your Feelings

Feelings are part of every experience you have:

• The excitement of your first school dance.

• The sadness when thinking about someone close to you who has died.

• The pride at receiving the Girl Scout Silver Award.

• The disappointment of not being invited to a friend's party.

• The happiness of being selected for the math team.

• The anger at being blamed for something you didn't do.

Feelings can change from one day to the next, sometimes from one minute to the next. They affect the way you think about yourself, the way you sound, and the way you react to others. Feelings are often expressed in "body language"—your posture, your facial expressions, and your gestures.

You may think that your feelings don't show, but your voice or your hands or your eyes may give them away. It often helps you and the people you deal with to express your feelings openly and honestly.

You may be able to use some help in getting in touch with your feelings and expressing your needs. The activities on the next page will help you bring your feelings into focus.

Handling Your Fears

Some feelings are more difficult to deal with than others. Fear is one of those—a common emotion that often clouds our thinking and causes us to feel isolated. Fear takes many forms: "fear of war," "fear of heights," "fear of bringing your report card home," "fear of becoming seriously ill," "fear of delivering an oral report in school." Interestingly, fear is always based on something that could happen in the future. Rarely is fear based on something that is happening at that moment. Keep in mind you are not alone in your fears. Many others share the same or similar fears.

HERE ARE SOME ACTIVITIES TO HELP YOU IDENTIFY AND COMMUNICATE YOUR FEELINGS.

▲ ACTIVITIES:

1. Using a large sheet of paper and color markers, jot down anything that enters your mind during ten minutes: Express your thoughts or feelings in words or pictures. Work rapidly without concern for grammar or neatness. After ten minutes, look at what you have written, and try to make sense of your thoughts. If you do this activity in a group, discuss your feelings with others. (Each person's sheet is bound to be very different.)

2. Work with a partner and take turns recording each other's words in a free association activity. Your partner calls out a word from a list of ten or more that she creates. After each one, you write the first word or phrase that comes to mind. After you both complete the activity, examine your thoughts as you did in the previous activity.

3. Think about situations that have occurred recently in which you could have communicated better. In your journal, write "I" messages for those situations. If you feel comfortable, discuss them with the person involved.

4. Each person in a group thinks about something she is afraid of or worried about, but doesn't usually talk about. Everyone then writes down her fear and puts it in a paper bag. (No name should be written on the paper.) Then, each person takes a turn reading a fear out loud for everyone to discuss. Nobody else will know who the fear belongs to, even if someone pulls her own. It is helpful to talk your fears over with someone else.

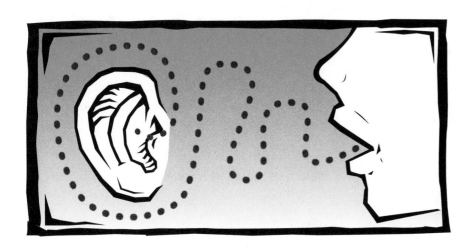

Conflict Resolution

Everyday conflicts are a fact of life. Conflict resolution is a way of working out problems between people. Following are some basic steps in conflict resolution.

1. Identify the Problem

All persons involved in the conflict meet to discuss exactly what the issue is. Each party should see the conflict as a problem to be solved. They define the problem, label it, write it down. If necessary, an outside, objective person can be brought in as facilitator. She will lead the discussion and take notes. In some cases, the facilitator can be the decision-maker. In most cases, however, the parties will arrive at a resolution by the end of the process.

2. Listen to Each Side of the Conflict

Each side takes turns discussing its point of view. One person speaks at a time and everybody else listens.

3. Identify Possible Solutions

Each side offers suggestions on how the conflict can be resolved. The facilitator writes down all suggestions.

4. Respond to Suggestions

In turn, each side reacts to the suggestions of the other side. They may reach agreement by reviewing their comments, discussing and analyzing the information, and convincing each other.

5. Reach a Compromise

The goal is to reach a decision that all parties can accept. The facilitator helps the group work out a compromise or helps them start over and work on a new solution.

Practice the five steps of conflict resolution by working out an actual family or group problem.

FRIENDS

During the transition to adulthood, as you and many young people like you seek more and more independence from parents or guardians, friends play a more central role in your life. You and your friends may help each other work out problems and cope with crises.

WORKING OUT PROBLEMS WITH FRIENDS

In a healthy friendship, both people give and take equally—the friendship is not one-sided. If things always went right in the world, all of our friendships would be balanced and there would never be a need to confront or cope with a changing relationship. But that isn't always the case. Relationships with friends are often like the waves of the ocean: they push forward, they pull back, they shift, they swirl, sometimes they even crash. You may recognize some of the following friendships. What advice would you give each writer?

The Selfish Friend

"My best friend and I make plans to go somewhere or do something together, but if a boy asks her out on a date, she always cancels her plans with me. This has happened many times. She always puts boys ahead of our friendship."

Your Advice: _____

_____

_____

Comments: This is an easy way to lose the trust of a good friend. Friends should be able to depend on each other. The message this person has given her friend is that she places more importance on her relationship with her boyfriend. Many adult women say that the friendships they formed with girls during high school have lasted into their adult years, yet they can't even remember some of the boys they were once interested in.

The Clinging Friend

"I like my friend very much, but since we've started a new school, she hangs around me all the time. She won't give me a chance to make any new friends. She monopolizes my time. If I tell her I'd like to spend some time with someone else, she acts hurt."

Your Advice: _____

_____

_____

Comments: The clinging friend has not had an easy adjustment to her new school. She finds it difficult to take the initiative and form new relationships. Listening to each other is a good way to begin to face the real issues here.

The Jealous Friend

"I have a friend who has helped me in many situations. But recently she's been talking about me behind my back. I just got the clarinet solo part in the spring concert, and she's been telling everybody that I didn't deserve it, that the teacher gave it to me instead of her because I tutor the teacher's son after school."

Your Advice: _____

_____

_____

Comments: This person should talk to her friend directly to make sure that what she heard is accurate. It also sounds as if the friend may be angry, perhaps over something that has nothing to do with the clarinet solo. She should get her "jealous" friend to speak openly to her about her true feelings. This situation calls for honest communication.

The "Boy" Friend

"There's this boy in my Spanish class. We're both interested in old cars. His father just purchased a 1965 Mustang, and he wants me to help him work on it. He's really cool and we like each other as friends, nothing more. But everybody keeps telling me that boys and girls can't just be friends without it turning into something more."

Your Advice:

_____

_____

_____

Comments: Many people cannot imagine boys and girls establishing friendships without some underlying romance creeping in. These people have been proven wrong quite often. Girls and boys can form close, long-lasting friendships, and often they are based on mutual interests.

The Friend of a Different Race

"My best friend is white. We've been friends for five years. Now people are telling me that since we are both older, it is normal for us to grow apart and spend more time with people of our own race. So far, we have not grown apart."

Your Advice:

_____

_____

Comments: These friends may never grow apart unless they allow themselves to be influenced by other people's negative, racist comments. True friendship has no color boundaries.

GANGS

Gangs are highly structured groups of young people that have codes of behavior, honor, and discipline. Adolescents turn to gangs for companionship, protection, and respect. People who have researched gangs say that they exist as an outlet for adolescent rage directed at authority figures, schools, parents, rules of all kinds. Gangs often demand blind obedience, and outside loyalties are seen as a threat to the group. In some of the more violent gangs around the nation, members are punished if they decide to leave the gang. They can no longer act and think as individuals.

If you are approached to join a gang or are already part of one, consider that gangs can be dangerous and demanding. Think about what the idea of the gang holds for you. Ask yourself if you can't find a healthier outlet for your needs. Ask a trusted adult for help if you find yourself in a situation you can't handle.

▲ FOR DISCUSSION:

Why does a young person join a gang? What attraction do gangs hold?

When a Friendship

Jenny and Elisa have been best friends for years. When they were younger, they used to spend all their time at each other's houses, riding bikes, and playing games. In middle school, they were inseparable, and when they weren't together, they were on the phone with each other. When Jenny and Elisa were in the ninth grade, they started going to dances with boys, and that gave them even more to talk about! By their sophomore year, they both were dating, going to parties, shopping, playing soccer, and doing all kinds of things that typical teenagers do for fun. Then, last summer, everything suddenly changed.

One Saturday afternoon, Jenny and Elisa and a group of friends from school went to the creek to go swimming. After an hour or so, one of the guys showed up with rope to make a swing. He tied the rope around a tree branch, then climbed down on the rope to swing out over the water and jump. Several others did the same thing, and then Elisa decided to try it. As she grabbed onto the rope and started to swing, the knot loosened, and instead of falling into the water, Elisa slammed into the creek bank.

Elisa just lay there for a long time, not moving. Jenny stayed with Elisa while somebody else ran to get help. The paramedics came and took Elisa to the hospital, and they let Jenny

Changes: A Story of Two Friends

ride along. Elisa's parents met them at the hospital. After several days, a doctor told Elisa that she was paralyzed from the waist down.

Since that time, Jenny and Elisa have remained friends, but things are not the same. Jenny goes to a lot of clubs and dances at school, but Elisa has given up on most of these activities. Mostly Elisa doesn't feel much like going out. So much has changed for Elisa, including the way she now feels about herself and how she thinks others view her.

Elisa doesn't talk about her disability much, but Jenny knows there are times when Elisa feels left out. Jenny also feels helpless at times and guilty for what happened. Jenny wishes things were different, but she doesn't know what to do.

▲ **FOR DISCUSSION:**

How do you think a sudden disability would affect a long-term friendship? What could each girl do to make the friendship vibrant again? How can communication help bridge the gap in their friendship?

MENU

Chili
Moo Shu Vegetable
Pasta Salad
Butterscotch Brownies
Ice Cream Cake
Lemonade

CELEBRATE FRIENDSHIP— THROW A PARTY!

There's no better way to celebrate friendship than to have a party! Parties are wonderful for getting to know people better. You can have a party at your house or organize one at a park, beach, skating rink, swimming pool, movie theater, or some other place. (If you're having the party at a facility, such as a skating rink, you need to make arrangements with the management.)

Once you have your family's permission and support, you need to make a list of people to invite. You can send written invitations or verbally

invite people. Be sure to keep track of who's coming.

Make a list of all the things you'll need: Food, utensils, decorations, chairs, etc. After you get everything, do as much preparation as you can ahead of time.

After all, you want to be able to have fun at your own party.

Once you know how many people are coming, plan the menu. Will you serve cold food, hot food, or snacks? Figure out what types and how much food you will need.

Be sure to socialize with all of your guests as the party progresses. Introduce people to each other and encourage them to mingle.

It is important to have adults around when you are throwing a party. For instance, uninvited guests may try to crash the party, or people may bring alcohol or drugs. You don't have to tolerate this behavior—you can set the limits. If the people don't do as you ask, tell an adult about the situation. Then let the adult help you.

The main thing is to enjoy your time with your friends and help your friends enjoy themselves. That's why you're there, to celebrate friendship!

DATING

Dating can provide opportunities for fun, sharing, affection, maybe even love. Going to the beach or a movie, watching television, or going on a picnic—all can be great fun with a terrific date.

WHY DO PEOPLE DATE?

Through dating, girls can learn more about boys, what being in a relationship means, and what qualities are important in a partner. Dating can eventually help prepare an individual for choosing a spouse.

In some groups, dating is a way to gain status. For instance, a girl might date a boy because he's captain of the football team and very popular in school. Is this a good reason for dating someone?

Entering a relationship with a boy can be quite challenging because it's not always easy to understand how another person thinks or feels. At one minute the boy you like might seem like your best friend and at another he might ignore you because the "guys" are around. Or he may begin to demand more and more time with you or pressure you to do something you don't want to do.

Maintaining a group of friends with similar interests is important for your personal development and happiness. Even if you are dating a particular boy, make time for your other friends and never give up your hobbies or extracurricular activities just to make time for your "boyfriend."

FRIENDS

It's a wonderful feeling of comfort
and care
When friends are around you,
just being there
Never demanding and
never commanding
Just wanting to listen, or deepest
thoughts share.
At their houses I spend all my time
When I'm there, have a wonderful time
We stay up all night, make French toast
with new light
With them I'll be friends for all time.
The movies we watch never end
That's the fun of having such friends
From eight until dawn, the VCR's on
Then rewind and start over again.
Our clothes with each other we share
We brush out each other's hair
We share our wishes, our laundry
and dishes
With the knowledge friends always
are there.
We talk on the phone for long hours
Talk of T.V. shows, chip dip, and flowers
It's a good thing, we witnessed,
that we're
not long distance
Or the phone bill would mainly be ours.
Our hair color isn't the same
Nor our eyes burn the same color flame
But the visitors passing, call us
"sisters," so laughing
I say heck with our families' last names.

–Robyn Rae Ready, age 16,
Heart of Ohio Girl Scout Council,
Ohio

AT WHAT AGE DOES DATING BEGIN?

Some girls begin to date at a younger age than others. For some, dating may start at 12 or 13; others may begin at 16 or 17. There's no right time to start. Consider your own feelings and needs. How does your family feel about your dating?

HOW DO BOYS FEEL ABOUT DATING?

Boys, like girls, can feel pressured to date, worry about rejection, and are concerned about how they look and act. But boys often hide their emotions so you may not always know how they really feel. Also, boys may seem to be self-centered when they're actually feeling unsure of themselves. They want to make a good impression, they want to be accepted, and they want to be liked. Sometimes they do things because they think it's expected of them, not because they feel they're ready for the experience.

Boys don't like being used or manipulated. Treat them the way you want to be treated. Act interested only if you really are. Don't act interested in one boy just to meet his friend or to make someone else jealous.

What do boys look for in a date? Probably most of the same qualities girls want—someone who is friendly, considerate, intelligent, self-confident, attractive, kind, supportive, and has a good sense of humor.

Maintaining established relationships and building new ones will constantly be a part of your life. Being sensitive to others—respecting their needs, feelings, and rights so that you can operate in harmony and mutual understanding—is a lifelong challenge.

Everybody **SKILLS**

Everybody **FOR**
Is wearing certain clothes. **LIFE**
Everybody
Is doing certain things.
Everybody
Likes certain music.
Everybody
Is dying to be popular.
Everybody
Is not what I am.
What's wrong with everybody?

—C.E. Osborn, age 16,
Pacific Peaks Girl Scout Council,
Washington

Chapter 5

LIFE SUCCESS SKILLS

What are life success skills and why would anyone want to develop them? Life success skills are ways of managing aspects of your life so you feel comfortable with everyday challenges. Have you ever been on an amusement park "bumper car" ride? It's fun yet a bit unsettling as you experience unexpected bumps and thrills. Sometimes your individual path in life can feel like that amusement park ride. Life success skills can help you manage life's bumps and thrills.

Life success skills can also give you focus. Along with the benefits of a fast-paced "technology and information" society comes the need to focus your attention, time, money, etc. Too much information can be overwhelming. The media, computer networks, and people with facts at their fingertips can sometimes overload you with more than enough information. Life success skills can help you "filter" the information in a reasonable and healthy way.

Lastly, life success skills can help you define your values as well as encourage you to take responsibility for your own personal growth. You decide which life skills are important to you and which are worth developing. In fact, you may want to develop your own set of "life success skills" as you become familiar with those included in this chapter.

TAKING AN ACTIVE ROLE

As you get older, you will be faced with more adult decisions and responsibilities. Taking an active role in the management of your life can give you balance and a strong sense of self. Remember, though, that life skills are refined over the course of your life, so don't expect to master them in a day!

▲ FOR DISCUSSION:

With your troop, group, or friends, discuss which life success skills are meaningful to you. Identify the skills you would like to improve on.

LIFE SUCCESS SKILL #1: MANAGING YOUR TIME

Time management is the way you balance your life so it includes time for family, studies, friends, sports and fitness, religious activities, Girl Scouting, and other interests.

▲ ACTIVITIES:

1. Make a list of your major weekly responsibilities and activities.
2. Place them in order of importance.
3. Create a weekly time schedule. Do your most difficult or time-consuming tasks when your energy level is the highest.

Take the example of Madeline Ginzburg. Madeline is taking some difficult classes at school, including two honors classes. She plays volleyball on her school team, is preparing for her Bat Mitzvah celebration (the initiation rite for Jewish girls), belongs to Girl Scouts, and watches her younger sister two days a week after school. Madeline is having a hard time planning her week so that she even has time to eat. She wants to take an aerobics class, but she doesn't know how to add it to her schedule. Also, she's so tired most of the time.

Do you recognize a bit of yourself in Madeline? If so, you can manage your time better by prioritizing your activities. Begin by discovering what time of day you have the most energy. Then, experiment with your time schedule.

LIFE IS

Sleep is like a rainbow,
the colors of the world.
Dreams are like rivers,
with endless bends and swirls.
A wishing star is a flaming jewel,
placed high up in the sky.
The clouds are wild horses,
running by and by.
Anger is a monster,
out to hurt and kill.
Sadness is a spring evening,
made cold with winter's chill.
Peace is like an angel,
a gift from up above.
The world is like a child,
for us to hold and love.
Life is an endless battle,
not one to give or take.
The armies of this war are
great love and awful hate.

–Mandy Jenkins, age 14,
Heart of Ohio
Girl Scout Council,
Ohio

LIFE SUCCESS SKILL #2: HANDLING STRESS

Stress is a part of life, and handling stress is an important skill to learn. Here are some examples of stressful situations:

• Meeting new people.

• Arguing with your best friend.

• Taking difficult school courses.

• Going on your first date.

• Trying out for a team, a scholarship, etc.

• Attending family celebrations.

Yes, even happy events can be stressful. You can experience the same symptoms—sweaty palms, nervous stomach, anxiety—during happy events as you experience during challenging events.

Test-taking is a common source of stress for teens. Test anxiety stems from self-doubt. You may have studied well for a test, but you're not sure of your ability to perform well at test time. Serious self-doubt makes it difficult to focus on the exam.

How do some girls conquer test anxiety?

"I close my eyes, take in a couple of deep breaths, and count to five very slowly. This helps me empty my mind of all thoughts."

"I make sure I get a good night's sleep. No staying up half the night cramming."

"My anxiety was caused by worry about what others might think if I failed. I used to put my reputation on the line for every test. Then I decided that no one test was worth all that."

APPROACH NEW THINGS WITH AN OPEN MIND

ASHLEY'S UPSET ABOUT HAVING TO ATTEND A FAMILY FUNCTION...

BUT SHE HAD NO WAY OF KNOWING SHE'D MEET BRAD, AUNT JANE'S NEIGHBOR, AT THE FAMILY PARTY.

Teenage Stress Scale

Below is a list of teenage "stressors," life events that are stressful. Have you experienced any of these stressors in your life? Give each event a stress value—decide whether it was a high-, medium-, or low-stress event.

Stressor	High	Medium	Low
1. Parents getting divorced or separated.	____	____	____
2. Living in a dangerous neighborhood.	____	____	____
3. An alcoholic, drug-addicted, or seriously ill family member.	____	____	____
4. Bad relationship with parent/guardian.	____	____	____
5. Parent/guardian being unemployed.	____	____	____
6. Moving to a new neighborhood or attending a new school.	____	____	____
7. Experiencing racial or other forms of discrimination.	____	____	____
8. Experiencing sexual harassment.	____	____	____
9. Having a disability.	____	____	____
10. Breaking up with a close friend.	____	____	____
11. Weight or size problems.	____	____	____
12. Failing a subject or grade in school.	____	____	____
13. Trouble with a teacher/principal.	____	____	____
14. Starting to date.	____	____	____
15. Starting menstruation.	____	____	____
16. Being pressured to be involved with alcohol or drugs.	____	____	____
17. Competing in a contest or audition.	____	____	____

I'm not a child anymore,
I can do it on my own.
I'm not an adult yet,
I can't drive myself to school.
I need to express myself,
Were your bell-bottoms so much better
than my flannel?
I like this kind of music,
What's wrong with it?
I'm not a "model child,"
So what? Were you?
I'm not like everyone else,
You needed to have your own
identity, too.
You're too overprotective,
Did you think I'd get mugged at the
mall with eight other people?
I need my privacy,
The "knock, Please" sign on my door is
there for a reason.
I'm not trying to leave home,
I just need my space.
You underestimate me,
I can choose good friends without help.
Please try to understand,
I'm not like you, I'm like me!

–Amanda Schroepfer, age 14,
Delaware-Raritan Girl Scout Council,
New Jersey

Although there are outward signs of stress—biting fingernails, being angry, or having trouble sleeping—stress is experienced inside of you.

Many teenagers bottle up feelings and do not seek out someone who can listen and offer advice. Stress can build up until physical and mental health suffers. Research has shown that stress can make you vulnerable to disease. Eating disorders, depression, feelings of suicide, and drug addiction, too, can all result from heavy stress. Everyone needs an outlet for stress.

How you relax or whether you relax at all has a lot to do with your ability to reduce stress. If you find that even your Saturdays and Sundays are frantic days, create some way to rest. Perhaps you can take a break and do something that's different and enjoyable to you. Find time to experience simple pleasures like getting together with friends, taking a long walk, or visiting a museum or the zoo.

WRONG WAY

WHO DO YOU THINK YOU ARE, BLOWING THAT FOUL SMOKE IN MY FACE?

LIFE SUCCESS SKILL #3: SPEAKING UP FOR YOURSELF

The way you interact with others is important to your well-being and success in life. If you don't let others know how you feel, you may end up accepting what other people dish out. On the other hand, aggressive behavior fosters anger and hostility, and distances you from others.

Speaking up for yourself in an assertive, respectful way is your best alternative. It is the ability to state how you feel honestly without anger or hostility.

You have a lot to gain by speaking up. It raises your self-esteem and gives you a voice in the group, but it might take practice. Girls are often trained to take a passive role.

How can you be more assertive? Try these activities:

• Watch other people who you think are assertive. Try to model your behavior after theirs.

• Pay attention to the times when you are not assertive and when you are assertive. In which situations are you comfortable being assertive?

• Imagine yourself being assertive or think about an instance when you were assertive. Consider how good you feel when you stand up for your rights.

• Act out being assertive by role-playing with friends.

• Practice being assertive in everyday situations. The more you practice, the easier it gets.

Get together with friends and create skits showing assertive, aggressive, and passive behaviors. Put on these skits for others. These are some situations you can use:

• The smoke from someone's cigarette is going in your face.

• Someone gets a well-done hamburger, when she ordered it medium-rare.

BETTER WAY

NEXT TIME, WHY NOT TRY THIS:

"EXCUSE ME; WOULD YOU MIND HOLDING YOUR CIGARETTE AWAY FROM ME? THE SMOKE IS GOING IN MY FACE."

• Someone is standing in line at the movie theater and another person cuts in front of her.

Remember that your assertive response may not always get you what you want. For instance, the store may refuse to refund your money for a defective product. However, you will still benefit from being assertive—it feels good to stand up for yourself!

SPEAKING OUT AGAINST SEXUAL HARASSMENT

Leslie hated going to her locker each day. There were two boys who hung out there just waiting for her to appear. One day one of them had actually

▲ FOR DISCUSSION:

Identify the types of sexual harassment you or your friends may have experienced. How did you respond? How would you respond if you had a second chance?

touched her breast and then said "excuse me" in an exaggerated voice. The other one laughed. She didn't know what to do.

Some sexual harassment is violent or physically aggressive. If you are being touched by boys in the hallway or

▲ ACTIVITY:

Role-play a situation where a girl is the victim of sexual harassment. Prepare two or three different endings and, with your audience, discuss each one.

while you're standing at your locker, or if a boy tries to touch you or move very close to you on the bus, this is sexual harassment. Sexual harassment can also take the form of verbal comments. No one—child, adolescent, or adult—has a right to address you with unwelcome sexual comments, or to treat you in a sexual way that makes you uncomfortable. Tell the person who is harassing you to stop. If the behavior continues or if you find it too difficult to assert yourself, report the behavior to school authorities and your parent or guardian.

Leslie went to her school counselor, and the two boys in question were given a choice of suspension or taking a six-week sexual-harassment awareness training course for teens sponsored by a women's group. If she hadn't spoken out, they might have continued their behavior with her or with other girls.

LIFE SUCCESS SKILL #4: STAYING SAFE

FIRST AID

Basic first aid is an important skill for anyone to know, and if you are ever left to care for young children, it's a skill you must have. Imagine these scenarios:

• You are baby-sitting. The baby is playing with a teddy bear and suddenly starts choking. She has swallowed an eye from the bear. She stops breathing. What do you do?

• Your brother is in the kitchen getting a snack while you do your homework. Suddenly you hear a scream. Instead of just getting the apple, he decided to slice it with a knife and cut his finger. What do you do?

Emergency first aid is taking care of life-threatening needs, such as bleeding, stopped breathing, poisoning, and shock.

In first aid, your best tools are calm thinking, soap and water, a basic first-aid kit, an emergency number to call for assistance (in most cases 911), plus your local poison-control number. You should know how to call for help, whether at home or on a trip.

PERSONAL SAFETY

Ever since you were young, you've probably learned many ways to protect yourself: Stay away from strangers; never hitchhike; don't walk home alone at night; report any suspicious or strange-looking person. All these safety rules are important to know, but

▲ ACTIVITIES:

1. Put together your own first-aid kit. (See *Safety-Wise* for suggestions.)
2. Take a first-aid and CPR course. The American Red Cross, the American Heart Association, or your local hospital or fire department may offer courses. Some hospitals offer courses for baby-sitters.
3. Make a poster that illustrates emergencies and first-aid techniques.

staying safe is a lot harder than watching out for the shifty-eyed stranger. Statistics show that most often young people are harmed or abused by someone they know and trust.

It's important to know how to avoid potentially dangerous situations at home, at school, in public places, on the street, and when baby-sitting. It's equally important to know how to say "no" to someone who tries to force you to do anything against your will. Saying "no" is especially hard when you feel threatened or if you know the person.

Let's take a look at the experiences of Liz, Kate, Malaika, and Susan and see how they handled their situations. Discuss what you would have done. Then, read the advice given.

Liz

After an evening of shopping at the mall, Liz and Keiko decided they would separate in the last hour before the stores closed and meet at the main entrance at 9:30 P.M. On her way to Green's Shop, Liz noticed uneasily that one particular man, with curly red hair, always seemed to be around. Yet the man was well dressed and didn't appear sinister. Liz put it out of her mind as she turned into Green's. She selected a pair of shoes and paid just before closing time. She then set out to meet Keiko back at the other end of the mall. Strolling past the now-closed shops, she felt a surge of fear when she spotted the red-haired man walking behind her. The mall had quickly become deserted and Liz was feeling panicky. What are Liz's options? What could she have done earlier to avoid her present predicament?

One of the most important safety tips is to avoid placing yourself in a potentially dangerous situation. Liz and Keiko shouldn't have separated at a time when they might well be alone in the mall. Liz should have paid attention to her first fears. Looks are not a good basis for determining good or bad intentions. Liz could have told someone in the shoe store about her worries. Even now, Liz can still protect herself by walking quickly or even running to another person in the mall. And if she really feels threatened, she shouldn't feel embarrassed about screaming for help.

LIZ AND KEIKO AT THE MALL...

"NO... I DON'T THINK THAT'S SUCH A GOOD IDEA. IT'S GETTING TOO LATE TO BE ALONE."

"IT'S GETTING LATE, SO LET'S SPLIT UP TO GET ALL OUR SHOPPING DONE."

Kate

When Mr. Anderson, the father of the child Kate was baby-sitting for, came home drunk, he insisted on driving her home. Kate was afraid to be rude, so she did not object to his driving her home. What could Kate have done?

Kate should have called her parents and requested that they pick her up or told Mr. Anderson she would be more comfortable taking a taxi. Mr. Anderson was in no state to drive her home safely. Never let the risk of hurting someone's feelings make you take chances with your own life.

Malaika

On her way home from school one day, Malaika stopped to chat with her neighbor Steve, who was home from work to accept the delivery of a new piano. Malaika had known Steve since she was five years old, so she wasn't concerned when he invited her in to see the new piano. While they were sitting down at the piano, Steve leaned very close and touched her thigh. When Malaika pulled back very startled, he told her it was an accident and not to tell anyone. What could Malaika have done?

Once Steve touched her, Malaika should have forcefully said "no" and run out of his house. Malaika should *not* keep this a secret, but should tell an adult she trusts. No one has a right to touch you or force themselves on you in any way. Trust your own instincts with regard to "accidental" touching and never feel guilty or somehow to blame.

Susan

Sometimes a situation arises where you become concerned about the personal safety of a friend or relative. You can play an important role in safeguarding the well-being of others. You may even save a life.

....

▲ ACTIVITY:

With your troop or group, make a list of places or situations—for example, at home, on a date, baby-sitting, or in the street—where young people might have to deal with personal safety. Then, prepare personal safety tips.

....

Susan knew that Rachel had been feeling more and more unhappy. It seemed that Rachel was dissatisfied with just about everything—family, friends, and school. She was extremely moody and withdrawn. Susan noticed that many of the friends and activities that had brought them so much enjoyment seemed no longer to mean anything to Rachel. Susan felt that once summer vacation began, she could coax her friend out of her depression, but lately she was wondering whether Rachel's mood might be really serious. Some of Rachel's comments frightened her, especially when Rachel said that "everything might be better if it were just all over." What can and should Susan do?

Susan is right to be afraid for her friend. She is getting signals that the situation may be very serious. Rachel might even be contemplating suicide. Many times friends are the first to recognize that things are getting out of hand. Susan should seek help by telling a family member, teacher, guidance counselor, health or crisis-intervention professional, or member of the clergy. Often a potential suicide victim is indirectly asking for help when she or he gives clues about feelings of despair and suicidal thoughts. Susan's concern and follow-up might save a life.

LIFE SUCCESS SKILL #5:
EARNING AND MANAGING MONEY

Celia, age 13, wanted to earn money to pay for a Girl Scout trip to Savannah. She was finding that financial independence was pretty difficult. She was too young for most of the jobs advertised for teens, so she brainstormed a list of jobs she might be qualified for. Since Celia really liked animals, she decided to start a pet-walking service. She called it "Paws to Walk."

Soon Celia realized she needed to manage the money from her animal-care business. First, she needed to keep a record of everything she made and everything she spent. Celia's mom suggested that she make a budget that would help her organize her money and keep track of how she spent it. (See the next page for a sample budget.)

To do this, Celia estimated her income for the month. She wrote down her "fixed expenses," those she had no choice about. They were the same each week, necessary expenses like school lunches and bus money. They might not be fixed if she could walk instead of ride the bus or take lunch from home instead of buy it at the cafeteria.

Then she estimated what her "flexible" expenses might be. These expenses varied from week to week. They were expenses for entertainment, small purchases, gifts. After adding those items up, she decided that the amount not spent could be put into savings, or better yet, savings could be put down as a fixed expense. That way she was sure to save each week.

CARPENTER

Career
Focus

What would I do?
If you were a "rough carpenter," you'd usually work outdoors building frames for the foundations of bridges, highways, or houses. If you were a "finish carpenter," you'd build cabinets and furniture, fit windows and doors, or lay floors. In either situation, you'd use tools to shape, saw, and connect wood.

Where would I work?
You'd work on construction sites, inside buildings, in factories or in small woodworking shops. You'd usually start by working for a contractor or a single organization. Eventually, you might become your own contractor.

What skills and education/training would I need?
You would need manual dexterity as well as a sense of precision and an understanding of mathematics and physics. A high-school diploma is helpful to start, but then you'd need to complete a union-contractor apprentice program, which takes about four years.

Interest Patch Link: Artistic Crafts; Folk Arts.

Create your own budget. For one month, keep a record of how much you spend and how much you earn (from allowance, part-time job, etc.). Create a budget for the next month based upon what you think your income will be. Try to stay within the budget. Record how much you actually spend. If you're spending too much, readjust your budget and try to stay within it for another month.

Your personal monthly budget could look something like this:

MONTHLY BUDGET

INCOME

	Estimated	Actual
Allowance	$_____	$_____
Earnings	$_____	$_____
Other income (gifts, bank interest on savings, etc.)	$_____	$_____
TOTAL INCOME	$_____	$_____

(To get your total income, add lines 1, 2, and 3.)

FIXED EXPENSES (EXPENSES THAT USUALLY STAY THE SAME)

	Estimated	Actual
Transportation	$_____	$_____
Troop dues	$_____	$_____
Other	$_____	$_____
TOTAL FIXED EXPENSES	$_____	$_____

FLEXIBLE EXPENSES (EXPENSES THAT VARY FROM DAY TO DAY)

	Estimated	Actual
Food	$_____	$_____
Clothing	$_____	$_____
Gifts and donations	$_____	$_____
Entertainment	$_____	$_____
Other	$_____	$_____
TOTAL FLEXIBLE EXPENSES	$_____	$_____

	Estimated	Actual
Savings	$_____	$_____
TOTAL EXPENSES, INCLUDING SAVINGS	$_____	$_____

LIFE SUCCESS SKILL #6: BECOMING A RESPONSIBLE CONSUMER

Are you a consumer? Do you: Buy groceries? Shop for your own clothes? Shop for personal-care products? Buy fast food? Use public transportation? Pick out gifts for friends and family?

If you answered "yes" to even one of these items, you are a consumer.

Advertisers recognize the power of teen consumers. They target commercials to your age group and strategically place products where you're likely to see them (such as the candy display at the supermarket checkout).

Manufacturers are trying to get you to buy, buy, buy, and to feel like you have to have whatever it is they are selling (see page 49). So, how do you become an effective consumer, one who feels confident about her choices?

First, read labels. Then evaluate the product for yourself. Next, don't be an impulse buyer, that is, someone who sees a product and buys it immediately. Manufacturers make a lot of money on this type of shopper. Before buying, compare products, read consumer publications, or ask people for endorsements. Finally, don't believe everything you hear about a product. One study, for example, found that when kids evaluated sneakers, the most expensive, trendiest ones were rated the most uncomfortable.

─────────────────────────

▲ TO CONSIDER:

Have you ever bought something because it was the "in" item to buy, then regretted spending your money on it?

─────────────────────────

FINANCIAL PLANNER

What would I do?
You'd help individuals and/or groups analyze their financial needs, then develop a strategy for investment or management of money.

Where would I work?
You might work for an investment corporation, a bank, or an insurance company. Or you might work for yourself and develop your own client base. In any case, you might lead workshops run by schools, libraries, or corporations.

Career Focus

What skills and education/training would I need?
You'd need to be skilled at working with numbers and budgets. You'd also need to be analytical and detail-oriented. Most employers want someone who has a college degree in finance, marketing, accounting, or economics. A master's degree or knowledge of such areas as insurance, taxes, and securities are also helpful.

Interest Patch Link: **Money Management.**

LIFE SUCCESS SKILL #7: PREPARING FOR A SATISFYING CAREER

B. LaRae Orullian,
National President
of Girl Scouts of
the U.S.A.

As National President of Girl Scouts of the U.S.A., B. LaRae Orullian serves as volunteer leader of the world's largest organization for girls. She also manages a successful career in the banking industry as chair of the board of the Women's Bank, N.A., in Denver, Colorado. In addition, Ms. Orullian lends her leadership skills to many civic and charitable causes.

What do you want to do when you become an adult? You don't have to come up with an answer right now, but it is time to ask yourself some leading questions: What are my talents and interests? Am I college-bound or not? Which skills should I be developing now to prepare me for a career?

Girls who set out on career paths have the benefit of more choices down the road. Life for most women does not follow a fairy tale format. You need to take responsibility for the type and quality of life you want, and not depend on anybody else to get it for you. Otherwise, you cast your fate to the wind.

Career Focus

The career focus sections found throughout this handbook can provide you with a variety of interesting jobs to explore. Note the different training and educational backgrounds required for different careers. Think about which types of work sites you would find most exciting.

▲ ACTIVITY:

What rewards do you hope to get from your job or career? Indicate on the chart below how you feel about certain aspects of your future job or career.

	Very Important	Important	Somewhat Important	Not Important
To be creative	☐	☐	☐	☐
To be challenged	☐	☐	☐	☐
To have a leadership role	☐	☐	☐	☐
To be adventurous	☐	☐	☐	☐
To be part of a team	☐	☐	☐	☐
To be the boss	☐	☐	☐	☐
To be well paid	☐	☐	☐	☐

Now, think about how you could prepare to meet the needs you have just indicated. For example, if it is important for you to be challenged and earn a good income, how would you prepare yourself for each? Which jobs could bring you these two rewards? Would those jobs satisfy you?

Although you make decisions all the time, sometimes you have to decide about something important. Perhaps you do well in math and are deciding whether to join the math club. Or, if you are a good art student, you may need to decide whether to take advanced art courses. Maybe you have the opportunity to get an internship, to join a sports team, or to further your skills in other ways. If you are faced with a tough decision, try the following decision-making steps:

1. **Figure out what the *real* issue is.** Identify the problem that requires a decision. Is the issue: which club should I join? Or: should I join a club at all?

2. **Gather information** to help arrive at a decision. Think about your feelings, values, goals, and interests. Talk to people you trust or visit the library to get some facts. Stop by the club, for instance, that you are thinking about joining.

3. **List the possible decisions** you could make.

4. **Look at the positive and negative aspects** of each decision. Weigh those aspects. For example, a strong negative (my best friend will never speak to me again) should carry more weight than a weak positive (it will be fun for a couple of hours). Also, think about the effect your decision will have on others.

5. **Make a decision** after you've considered all the information.

6. **Act on your decision.** For example, join the math club.

7. From time to time, **reevaluate your decision.** As circumstances change, you may need to redo the decision-making process.

GATHERING INFORMATION

LISA IS INTERESTED IN THEATER.

IDEAS FOR LISA TO CONSIDER:

• JOIN THE SCHOOL DRAMA CLUB.
• TAKE AN ACTING CLASS.
• TALK TO A PROFESSIONAL.
• EXPLORE RELATED FIELDS: LIGHTING, MAKE-UP, SET OR COSTUME DESIGN.

Reaching Goals

Once you've made the decision to do something, you'll need a plan to make it happen. Try to achieve your goal by breaking it down into steps:

1. Identify the goal.
For example: "to exercise three times a week."

2. Monitor behavior.
For one week, don't do anything differently, just observe how you spend your time. Keep a written record. For example: "Today, I spent one hour after school talking to my friend on the telephone."

3. Review your week's behavior and develop a plan to reach your goal.
For example: "Instead of talking on the telephone, I could suggest to my friend that we take an exercise class."

4. Reward yourself.
For example: "After exercise class, my friend and I can hang out at my house for a while."

If you have not been able to reach your goal, try to figure out what happened. Were you striving for an unrealistic goal? Were you not motivated enough to accomplish your goal? Was your goal not important enough for you to apply a great deal of effort? If you are still interested in pursuing your goal, revise your plan and start again!

Making Decisions to Be Environmentally Aware

Young people across the country are leading the way in environmental awareness. They are demonstrating the power of groups and individuals to care for the earth. As a Girl Scout, you already may have worked on an environmental service project or practiced minimal-impact camping.

● ●

What You Can Do as an Individual to Live Environmentally

≥ Walk

≥ Ride your bike

≥ Plant trees

≥ Put washers on leaky faucets

≥ Take short showers

≥ Turn off water when brushing your teeth

≥ Recycle paper as wrapping paper

≥ Use old jewelry to make new

≥ Recycle magazines by distributing them to others

≥ Donate used clothing

≥ Start a uniform swap in your Girl Scout service unit

≥ Keep the thermostat turned down in cold weather
and up in warm weather

≥ Repair and donate old toys

≥ Ask your parents to car-pool

≥ Start a community garden

● ●

I pledge to care for the earth. As a Girl Scout, my promise to obey the Girl Scout Law means that I will make a difference by using resources wisely and protecting and improving the world around me. I am a caretaker of this planet. I can make a difference now and for the future. I will strive to do my part for the earth in my daily life. I am part of solutions to environmental problems we face. I make this pledge knowing that caring for the earth is a lifetime project.

What Your Troop or Group Can Do to Care for the Earth

~ Coordinate an environmental service project.

~ Sponsor or set up an exhibit at an environmental fair.

~ Plan a minimal-impact camping trip.

~ Shop environmentally for all troop or group needs. Remember to precycle, recycle, and reuse.

~ See the Contemporary Issues book *Earth Matters: A Challenge for Environmental Action* for other activity ideas.

Lou Henry Hoover Memorial Sanctuary projects were established in 1944 by the GSUSA National Board of Directors as a living memorial to Lou Henry Hoover, wife of Herbert Hoover, former President of the United States. She was an active Girl Scout from her investiture by Juliette Low in 1917 to her death in 1943. She served twice as elected President of GSUSA and once as Honorary President.

During her years in Girl Scouting, Lou Henry Hoover worked enthusiastically to enlarge the scope of Girl Scout program in the out-of-doors. This interest is built into the design of Lou Henry Hoover Memorial Sanctuaries.

A Lou Henry Hoover Memorial Sanctuary is any natural area desig-nated by a council for the purpose of providing a setting where Girl Scouts can gain an understanding of the interrelationships of all forms of life. Girls must play a part in analyzing, planning, developing, and managing the site. The initial plan for development and management must cover a five-year period.

Career
Focus

PARK RANGER

What would I do?

You would protect and preserve the nation's forests and national parks. You might lead tours, hikes, or nature walks through the park. On any given day you might monitor and repair trails, rescue rock climbers, and give first aid. You'd also be the primary source of law enforcement within the parks and forests.

Where would I work?

Most of the time, your work site would be the park itself, although you might travel to other places such as schools or libraries for workshops.

What skills and education/training would I need?

You'd need to enjoy working outdoors, have expertise in hiking and camping, and be fit and healthy. You'd also need to be creative, resourceful, patient, and energetic. A bachelor's degree with an emphasis on ecology, botany, zoology, or geology is usually the minimum requirement. A master's degree is frequently an advantage in this competitive field.

Interest Patch Link: Orienteering; Hiking; Outdoor Survival; Eco-Awareness.

Happiness

*How often we wearily
Stumble through
A bit of happiness,
Without realizing it.
We've no sense at all!*

*–Janine Rinker, age 14,
Chipeta Girl Scout Council,
Colorado*

EXPLORING NEW INTERESTS AND ACTIVITIES

Chapter 6

THE VALUE OF RECREATION

Do you enjoy the roar of the crowd, the crack of the bat, and the camaraderie of the team? Do you like to sit quietly with a sketch book and pencil at the park? Do you enjoy the exhilaration that accompanies hiking up a steep trail? From team sports to the out-of-doors to the arts, music, or computers, Cadette Girl Scouts pursue many interests that make their lives exciting and fun. The purpose of this chapter is to suggest activities you could explore alone or with a group.

While educational and work-related activities certainly have a central place in your life, finding enjoyable activities for leisure time is important too. The combination of successful work and enjoyable leisure pursuits is vital for personal well-being. Recreational activities can lead to rewarding experiences and friendships and may become an important focus in your life, perhaps leading someday to a career.

Recreation gives you a refreshing and often needed break from your day-to-day schedule of school, work, household chores, and other demands. Pursuing a special interest adds balance to your life, and helps you get to know yourself better.

▲ ACTIVITY:

If you could have three gifts, which of the following would you choose?

• Trip to a foreign country
• Trip to the Olympics
• CD or tape collection
• Speed boat
• Scuba diving outfit
• Skis
• Rafting expedition
• Five years of music lessons and the instrument
• Library of books of your choice
• Season concert tickets
• A gourmet cook for a year
• Gold bracelet
• New wardrobe
• Pet dog
• Camera and equipment
• Plant collection
• Microscope
• Computer
• Season sports tickets
• One-year pass to your local movie theater

Hobbies

Some people develop their interests into hobbies. A hobby is any type of activity one does during leisure time for relaxation, for pleasure, to learn something new, or to develop a skill. A hobby can become a serious interest and may even lead to a career.

CHOOSING A HOBBY

Do you have a hobby? Do you have interests that can be turned into hobbies? For example, a love of horses could become a collecting hobby whereby you collect horse figures and photographs.

Complete the activity on the opposite page. What do your selections tell you about your interests? Ask some friends or family members to do this activity. Compare your answers with theirs.

If you are in the process of selecting a hobby and only have an idea about the hobby, do some research. Go to the library and look through books that deal with the subject. Also, try to find someone who has the same interest. Ask her to share information with you. Or join a club that is practicing that hobby.

IN THE WOODS

In the woods I like to be,
With the birds that build
their nests in the trees.
To be free to hike out under the sun,
My troop and me, we always have fun.
We search for signs of life everywhere,
And we hope we don't
meet up with a bear
We find flowers and ferns
wherever we go,
To find moss and lichens
we have to look low.
If we walk very quietly,
We may see a deer behind that tree,
Or a frog or a toad or a butterfly,
And when we do we'll always say, "Hi."
In the woods I like to be,
With the birds that build their
nests in the trees.
To be free to hike out under the sun,
My troop and me, we always have fun!

--Christine Neumann, age 16,
The Girl Scout Council of
Greater St. Louis, Missouri

Turning Hobbies into Careers

Your values, interests, and hobbies may lead you to a career. Many artists began as children with art hobbies. Many athletes began with games and sports hobbies. Considering the values, interests, and hobbies you have now, in what types of careers do you see yourself? See the examples in the chart below and add your own ideas.

Values	Interests	Hobbies	Possible Careers
Examples:			
Healthy living	Food, nutrition, health	Cooking	Nutritionist, chef, caterer, restaurateur, food writer, researcher, product demonstrator
Conservation of the natural environment	Animals, plants	Observing wildlife	Wildlife biologist, teacher, ranger, botanist, zoologist, veterinarian
		Nature photography	

When it comes to career choice, the important thing is to pay attention to your feelings about what you like doing. If writing is an activity you find exciting, for example, consider a career path where writing skills are used. Take time to get to know yourself and to recognize what you enjoy. And remember that your needs and interests change throughout your life.

Go Fly a Kite

There is a freedom of body and spirit in flying a kite, and it appeals to any age. You can share this interest with younger children, grandparents, or people your own age. Kite flying is a favorite American pastime, and many towns across the country hold annual kite-flying contests.

Actually, the sport of kite flying is centuries old in the Asian cultures. In Thailand, children fly kites painted and shaped as dragons, fish, owls, and other creatures. Their kite contests are very popular and competitive.

Consider building and decorating your own kite. Begin with simple methods using plywood for construction of the kite's foundation. Be creative in shaping and painting your kite.

You might enjoy kite flying as a solitary hobby or group activity. Steady winds and open spaces provide perfect conditions for kite flying. There will be good kite-flying days during any of the four seasons. How about organizing a community kite-flying day for neighbors of all ages? Check your library for books about the art of kite making.

Bird-watching

Bird-watching is a hobby that can be combined with hiking. Some parks have organized groups who go "birding," but with a pair of binoculars and a friend or two, you can get started on your own. (Remember to talk in low tones; birding is a quiet adventure!)

Start by learning about the birds common to your area. Find out their names, sizes, shapes, and colors, how they sound, and what their habits are. This makes it easier for you to recognize them.

Keep track of the different birds you see by recording their names or descriptions in a notebook. Serious "birders" keep a running list of different species they find in a lifetime. Some lists contain the names of several hundred species.

Enjoy the birds in your own backyard. Make a simple bird feeder and watch the birds as they feed. You can learn a lot about their interactions by observing their behavior.

Stargazing

Almost everybody has tried to find the Big Dipper in the night sky. Well, there is much more to learn about the fascinating topic of celestial bodies. The ancient Egyptians, American Indians, the Aztecs, and navigators from all cultures used the sky to create calendars, serve as a guide to their destinations, and make decisions about their lives. Harriet Tubman used the North Star to help lead her people out of the South and slavery.

The sky changes with the seasons as the earth rotates around the sun, and there is always something new to discover up there.

Try these stargazing activities:

1. Learn how to find directions from the sky. You might start by finding the North Star (also called Polaris).

2. Look for the Big Dipper and the Little Dipper. All the stars in the Big Dipper are very bright. The Little Dipper's stars are not as bright or easy to pick out.

3. Use a star chart to find constellations. Find the signs of the zodiac. Begin by looking for your own sign first.

4. Many of the planets are visible on clear nights. Can you find Venus? Mars?

ARTS-RELATED HOBBIES

Painting and Drawing

Since you can draw and paint using a wide range of materials, self-expression is limitless. You can choose from among various pens, different grades of lead and charcoal pencils, acrylic, watercolor, or oil paints and from among countless surfaces: Canvas, posterboard, cardboard, even rocks, shells, and fabric. And, of course, you can choose a computer screen as your canvas. Try using cotton balls, sponges cut in different shapes, leaves, and branches as painting tools.

You might try, as some artists do, keeping a sketchbook with you to "doodle" or sketch out ideas as they come to you throughout the day. Find images that inspire you: Nature, children, animals, buildings.

Photography

Photography is an interest that can grow with you through the years. You can take photos alone or with a group.

The first step is to learn all you can about your camera: How it works, how to care for it, how to load it with film, how to change its batteries, even how to take it apart. Then, begin by shooting with black and white film. Not only is it cheaper to buy and develop, but black and white film offers a unique means for experimentation.

Calligraphy

Calligraphy is the ancient art of fine handwriting or lettering. The Chinese and Japanese have practiced this art for many centuries. They use calligraphy to write poetry, letters, and entire books. In this country, handwriting used to be a school subject like reading, writing, and arithmetic. Before ballpoint pens were invented, people used to write with fountain pens, which enhanced the art of handwriting.

You can learn calligraphy by taking a class, getting instruction from a calligrapher, or reading a calligraphy book and practicing the lettering yourself.

Choose a subject each week and shoot only that subject. For example, shoot trees of different sizes and shapes. Other possible subjects are buildings, animals, signs, flowers, young children, and statues.

PHOTOGRAPHER

What would I do?
You would take and print photographs as well as coordinate photo sessions.

Where would I work?
You might work in a lab as a scientific photographer, in a factory as an industrial photographer, for a newspaper or magazine as a photojournalist, or in a studio doing portrait work.

What skills and education/training would I need?
You need thorough knowledge of photography equipment and processing as well as an understanding of what you are photographing. You also need an artistic eye, patience, and organizational skills. As for training, practical experience is the most important requirement. You can gain experience through an apprenticeship, a technical school, or a two- or four-year college.

Interest Patch Link:
Photography.

Career Focus

To become familiar with calligraphy:

1. Acquaint yourself with the different size pens in a calligraphy set. (This may mean purchasing a beginner's set.) Or, experiment with felt-tip pens of different thicknesses.

2. Practice holding the pens in your hand. Try writing with them. How do they feel? Some pen tips are thicker than others. What difference does that make in the lettering?

3. Look at samples of lettering. Some are fancy, elaborate styles. Roman, italic, uncial, and copperplate are a few. Select two or three styles you like, and practice them.

4. Select a style and write a favorite quote, poem, invitation, or letter.

Reading

Reading can be a lifetime love you take with you almost anywhere. Reading transfers you to the past, the future, to fantasy lands, and exotic places. You read about all kinds of people who get themselves in and out of situations. Through reading, you learn about life and about yourself.

Consider forming or joining a book club where members meet regularly to discuss a book the group has selected. Read some of the favorite books Cadette Girl Scouts have recommended: *Searching for Dragons*, *The Secret Garden*, *If I Should Die Before I Wake*, *I Know Why the Caged Bird Sings*, and *The Chronicles of Narnia*. If you like series books, read Janet Oke's series about women of the West, the Baby-Sitter series, and the Nancy Drew series.

Don't forget that reading does not have to be limited to novels, but can include magazines, nonfiction picture books, newspapers, and poetry.

Writing

Writing is a pursuit that can offer you a creative outlet, insight into yourself and others, and a release for your thoughts and feelings. Writing has such a personal nature that not everyone chooses the same format. Writing can take the form of a short story, a poem, a play, a humorous essay, or journal writing. Many writers, in fact, credit journal writing as the beginning of their writing careers. If writing is something you enjoy, why not submit something to your community or school newspaper or literary journal?

COMPUTERS

You are part of the computer generation. Computers and sophisticated software are part of our everyday lives.

Ask an older family member or friend how she wrote a report when she was in junior high school. Chances are she used a manual typewriter or wrote the paper by hand. She probably did the research in the library without computers to help find sources. Today, computer-driven technology has made writing research papers quicker and easier. You can even send homework assignments to teachers via electronic or E-mail.

MANAGEMENT INFORMATION SYSTEMS (MIS) ANALYST

What would I do?
You would work with computers, where you might develop software programs or oversee the use of that software. You'd work as part of a team, overseen by a manager.

Career Focus

Where would I work?
Almost anywhere! Banks, hospitals, universities, and airlines are among the most current users of this technology though many industries need MIS personnel. The cutting-edge jobs will be in interactive television and video-communications.

What skills and education/training would I need?
An inquiring, imaginative, and analytical mind coupled with a talent in problem-solving are great assets. You'd also need a college degree in electrical engineering, computer science, mathematics, or information systems, as well as knowledge of computer languages.

Interest Patch Link:
Computers; High-Tech Communications.

Are you familiar with the uses for computer technology? Look at the following list. If you have not yet tried to use or observe the following technology, see if you can find a friend or resource that will allow you access.

• Have you "talked" to friends electronically or used a computer bulletin board? You can do this if the computer is hooked up to a modem which transfers information across telephone lines.

• Do you use programs on CD-ROM, storage devices that can hold thousands of pages of information and video clips?

• Have you played video games? You can play games on a home computer, home television, or through a hand-held video device.

• Have you ever used a computer to look through a store catalog or to order a product?

• Have you watched a family member use an ATM (automatic banking machine)?

• Have you used a telephone equipped with voice mail: Press 1, Press 2, leave a message, etc.?

• Have you tried your hand at computer-generated graphics?

Can you add to this list? You will be better equipped for school and a career if you learn as much as possible about computers.

SPORTS AND OUTDOOR PURSUITS

WOMEN AND SPORTS— A LONG LEGACY

Women have been involved in sports since ancient times. Through art, there are records of women in the fifth century B.C. running track competitively. In the second century, they swam and participated in gymnastics. Women in Nordic countries hunted on skis in the 1500s, and women's wrestling was a popular sport in France during the 1800s. Nineteenth-century women athletes participated in sports dressed in skirts and corsets. Some played basketball on courts curtained off from public view. Early Girl Scout troops in Savannah played basketball competitively, and the results were listed in a regular newspaper column.

THE JUMP

What should I do?
What should I do?
Should I go over this jump?
I might get dumped!
The jump is so high!
Ten feet wide and up to the sky!
The ground of the ring is really wet!
It probably is as sticky as tar I bet!
My palms are sweating.
My heart is beating.
My blood is ice cold.
I am not really bold.
My horse is the wildest of the bunch.
He probably is mad because he got no lunch!
My instructor has just told me to go.
I really do not want to, "Oh, wait. Whoa!"
Over the jump we spring!
Higher than the fence of the ring!
I get into position to leave the ground.
Up, up, up, I go and I don't look down.
I jump and I hope my instructor is proud.
So high, I could almost grab a cloud.
I soar off into the sky.
"Look, I am trying to fly!"
Hey, wait! That was not so bad!
Wow! I am really glad!
We did not even feel a bump.
Can I please go for one more jump?

–Erin Yoder, age 14,
Girl Scouts of Delaware County,
Pennsylvania

TEAM SPORTS

You may have been involved in organized sports as a young child, or you may be part of a sports team right now. If so, your sports involvement has probably helped you develop physical and social skills.

Benefits of Playing on a Team

The benefits of playing a team sport do not stop with improved physical conditioning. Being a member of a team helps you establish friendships with people who share similar interests. Teamwork can also express the value of working with and accepting others. For example, team members learn it is not acceptable to look down on, tease, or exclude someone who doesn't play as well as they do.

If you have a disability, being involved in sports is especially beneficial. Sports involvement can offer you an understanding and acceptance of your body that other girls may not have. Being involved in a team sport can help you feel confident about your abilities.

Leadership

Playing on a team offers you an opportunity to practice leadership skills. While many teams are coached by adults, the players elect their own captains. Team captains try to:

• Build "team spirit."

• Assist other players in developing skills.

• Work with coaches and referees in determining rules and regulations.

Some girls do not enjoy the benefits of playing on a team because they are afraid they will not be good enough, or

that others will laugh at them and their abilities. You should remember that no one is automatically a "pro" and that with practice you can improve your skills. If you give yourself a chance, your confidence and comfort with the group will also improve. Participating in sports can encourage you to undertake new challenges in other areas of your life.

Other Ways to Participate

If you genuinely do not like to play team sports, you can still be part of a

team. Most athletic teams need scorekeepers or managers who help organize information and equipment.

If you have writing or photography skills, consider being a sportswriter or photographer for the school newspaper. As a journalist covering sporting events, you will get to know the players and coaches and become directly involved in the excitement of the game.

Coaching youngsters is a third way to participate in team sports. Working with young children can be particularly gratifying because you will help them develop athletic and social skills.

HOSTING YOUR OWN SPORTS TOURNAMENT

Planning the Tournament

Planning a tournament is an exciting activity you can do with your troop or group. In fact, it might be fun to host a tournament along with other Girl Scouts in your community.

First, consider the many details involved in planning a tournament. You need to check *Safety-Wise* and get clearance from your Girl Scout council to hold a sporting event. You must decide which sports will be played and who will be invited to compete. Will you challenge other Girl Scout troops or groups? Will girls form their own teams? Will the tournament be open to girls who are not Girl Scouts?

Secondly, you must decide when your tournament will take place. Will it be after school or on a weekend? Perhaps it will be during the summer.

Third, you must decide where the games will be played. Can you get permission to use the fields at your school? Can you play in a public park? Do you need to get a special permit to play in a public area?

CROSS-COUNTRY RUNNING

*Caring coaches
Running
Only fun
involved
Strength of the
body and mind
Super exercise
Running: My
favorite pastime
Years of training
and experience*

–Angela Gburek, age 15, Sybaquay Girl Scout Council, Illinois

Setting Up Committees

Deciding on the who, what, where, and when will provide your tournament with structure. Then, you will need to consider specific details such as rules and regulations, publicity, and fund-raising. It may be helpful to set up patrols or committees to handle these aspects.

The Rules and Regulations Committee

This committee will decide on the format of the tournament; for instance, will play be competitive or noncompetitive? If it is decided that play will be competitive, will it be single or double elimination? In single elimination, each team plays one game, with the winners playing against the other winners. In other words, once a team loses a game they are out of the competition. A double elimination tournament, on the other hand, allows each team to play at least two games before they are out of the competition. Or you can host a noncompetitive tournament with each team playing every other team.

In addition to deciding on format, the members of this group will be responsible for researching the official rules of the game. They will also contact people who might volunteer to be referees.

The Publicity Committee

This committee promotes the tournament to other Girl Scout troops and groups or to the whole community. They will be responsible for creating and distributing fliers and posters about "tournament day." One or two girls might also want to be photographers or reporters who cover practice sessions as well as the tournament.

The Money-Earning Committee

To host a tournament, you will need to know how much things cost. This committee is responsible for setting up a budget and raising money. Expenses might include: The cost of printing fliers, filing for permits, or hiring referees. Committee members should devise ways to raise money well before the tournament takes place. Also, you might want to consider selling food or drinks on the day of the tournament.

Planning and hosting an athletic tournament can be a lot of fun. It is a good chance to meet other Girl Scouts in your community and show others the opportunities provided by Girl Scouting.

CHOOSING A PHYSICAL ACTIVITY

Not only are physical activities fun, but they can feel exhilarating and offer important benefits to your body.

Choose activities that fit your schedule and interests. The chart (opposite page) includes a sampling of activities along with their fitness benefits.

Aerobics

Conditions heart and lungs; develops rhythm, agility, and coordination.

Swimming

Conditions total body; tones muscles; relaxes body.

Bicycling

Conditions heart and lungs; strengthens leg and back muscles.

Walking (brisk)

Lowers resting heart rate; improves oxygen consumption; reduces blood pressure.

Volleyball

Builds muscular strength, speed, power, hand-eye coordination, and agility.

Softball

Builds muscular strength, speed, agility, and coordination.

Running

Conditions heart and lungs; tones muscles; increases stamina.

Skating

Conditions heart and lungs; strengthens leg and thigh muscles.

Horseback Riding

Increases stamina; strengthens thigh and leg muscles; tightens abdominal muscles.

We come, individually,
the seeds of
a thousand flowers,
on a thousand crosswinds.
Some of us
come in
on the strong gusts of
winter's turmoil,
while others arrive on
a gentle summer's breeze.
Thistle or lily alike,
we all sprout,
shooting roots downward,
raising radiant petals to the
sun,
to form a brilliant garden,
that has no walls.

–Rebecca Rogers, age 15,
Abnaki Girl Scout Council,
Maine

HAVE YOU CONSIDERED ...WALKING!

Walking is one of the healthiest activities you can do at any age. A brisk walk pumps up the heart rate and keeps it working at its elevated rate. It tones hip, thigh, and leg muscles, and can give your upper body a workout, too. Walking helps you lose weight, increases the flexibility of your joints and muscles, and gives you more energy.

Walking programs take little organizing and no equipment except a sturdy pair of shoes. The walking groups described here can be easily adapted for your troop's or group's use. See the contemporary issues book *Developing Health and Fitness: Be Your Best!*, the accompanying health and fitness activity poster, and the video *Be Your Best!* for more ideas.

Walking with others can be fun and can give this form of exercise some structure. Here are some walking groups you can form with friends, family, and neighbors:

1. School Walkers: Discover several different but safe routes to school.

2. Speed Walkers: Meet after school and take the long way home. Walk as fast as you can—speed walk—and swing your arms rapidly, in pace with your feet.

3. Dog Walkers: Socialize with friends while exercising yourself and your dogs. Don't forget to keep up a steady pace!

4. Family Walkers: Combine with other families to walk in the evening or on weekends.

For all outdoor activities that involve walking in wooded or densely vegetated areas, remember to protect yourself from ticks that may carry Lyme disease. Always walk with a buddy, and let an adult, who is not with you, know where you intend to be.

HAVE YOU CONSIDERED ...HIKING!

The joy of hiking comes from being out-of-doors in a safe, natural, quiet environment. Quiet? If you listen attentively as you hike, you'll hear just how noisy nature can be. The next time you hike, stop for a minute, close your eyes, and try to identify the different sounds. You might hear a squirrel rustling through dried leaves, the wind gently blowing through the vegetation, or birds calling one another. What other natural sounds can you hear?

Good hiking opportunities exist in urban, suburban, and rural areas. Wear a sturdy pair of shoes or hiking boots and dress in layers you can shed. Temperatures can fluctuate throughout the day and with altitude. Some parks have guides that conduct hikes on nature trails.

HAVE YOU CONSIDERED ...BACKPACKING!

Backpacking is an overnight hiking trip where you carry your equipment on your back. You must be in good physical condition before you get on the trail. Don't plan to get in condition while on the trail. Carrying a pack up a steep slope or while walking in a downpour can be physically challenging. A positive attitude and sense of humor are real assets on wilderness travel.

To select an area in which to backpack, study a topographical map and plan your route carefully. Locate potential campsites and figure the distances between them. Plan your time for the slowest hiker in the group. Don't forget to consider the difficulty of the terrain and the amount of daylight you have. Allow enough time for setting up and leaving camp, meals, and rest stops.

Backpacking Tips

1. Carry no more than 20 percent of your body weight unless you are in excellent condition.

2. Dress in layers and don't forget to pack rain gear.

3. Take good care of your feet. Change your socks several times a day.

Inspect the route carefully for potential hazards such as stream crossings or ridges exposed to afternoon thunderstorms. Consider the weather conditions. Will it be hot and humid or cold and wet at a high elevation? Do you need to be concerned about insects or wild animals? Before setting out, check *Safety-Wise* for information on day and overnight trips.

While on the trail, drink plenty of fluids, not only at meal time but throughout the day. If you become dehydrated, the chances of getting heatstroke or altitude sickness increase. A hiker suffering from dehydration may have headaches, feel nauseated, or have muscle cramps.

Take time to enjoy sunrises and sunsets. Lie on your back and watch passing clouds. Listen to bird calls and watch soaring hawks. Look for signs of wildlife. Sketch, take pictures, write poetry. Practice minimal-impact camping and enjoy your wilderness experience!

Hiking guidebooks, trail guides, hiking clubs, park rangers, or guide services can help plan a backpacking trip. Some Girl Scout camps are adjacent to a state park or national forest.

Map and Compass Skills

Map and compass-reading skills are helpful to know for hiking and backpacking. As you learn to use a map and compass, you will gain important skills to plan complicated hikes and backpacking trips.

Following a Compass Bearing

A baseplate compass is recommended because it combines the features of a compass dial with those of a protractor, which measures degrees.

BACKPACKING

Beneath the starry skies in the Adirondack Mountains Cool breezes blow through the trees with the Killdeers crying in the meadows North Star shining bright it is a Great sight

—Tracy A. Moore, age 14, Connecticut Yankee Girl Scout Council, Connecticut

Suppose you want to walk from Point A to Point B:

1. Place your compass on the map. Connect your current map location (Point A) with your destination (Point B) using one of the long edges of your compass. Make sure the direction-of-travel arrow is pointing from where you are on the map to where you want to go, not the reverse. Otherwise, you will walk 180° in the wrong direction!

2. Rotate your compass dial until the orienting lines are parallel with the magnetic north-south lines on the map. (Ignore the magnetic needle). Check to see that north on the dial is pointing in the same direction as the north arrow on the map.

3. Remove your compass from the map. Hold the compass in front of you with the direction-of-travel arrow pointing the same way you are facing. While holding the compass in this position, rotate your body until the north end (red) of the magnetic needle is pointing toward north on the dial. You will now be facing in the direction of your destination.

If you wanted to walk to this destination, you would look up and pick out an object straight ahead of you. You would walk to the object and repeat Step Three as many times as necessary to reach your destination.

For more information on map and compass reading, see *Outdoor Education in Girl Scouting.*

Once you know how to read a map and use a compass, try leading your troop or group on a map walk around your community. Select eight to ten locations on the map. Determine your route and how much distance you will have to walk between points. First, "walk" the route by tracing your path with your finger. Once you feel you know the route, lead a real map walk around the neighborhood.

Whether you're exploring a new hobby, making a first attempt at a team sport, or developing an interest you've had since you were little, recreational pursuits can add dimension to your life. Through your pursuits, you become a more interesting person, learn about who you are, and have fun doing it!

Girl Scouts...
A combination of family and friends.
Girls Scouts...
Where fun never ends.
Girl Scouts...
Handbooks and patches.
Girl Scouts...
Uniforms and sashes.
Girl Scouts...
Sisters all around you.
Girl Scouts...
A part of you.

–Carissa Griffith, age 15,
Great Rivers Girl Scout Council, Ohio

RECOGNITIONS FOR CADETTE GIRL SCOUTS

Chapter 7

SELECTING ACTIVITIES AND RECOGNITIONS

As a Cadette Girl Scout, you engage in all kinds of activities such as designing a trail for the visually impaired, investigating careers, and learning photography. Not only do you enjoy the challenge and fun of these activities, but you get to earn Girl Scout recognitions.

Recognitions are designed to help you develop your skills to the fullest potential. Moreover, when you complete recognition requirements, you are entitled to receive a badge, pin, or patch as a symbol of your accomplishments.

You may be thinking: "So many of the activities seem interesting and appealing, how can I ever choose which recognition to work on?" The following guidelines may help you with your decisions:

• Choose activities based on your interests—not because a friend or your troop or an adult chooses one for you.

• Do not judge a recognition by its name. Read through a recognition's requirements prior to beginning any work. You may find a recognition with little "name" appeal to be just what you're looking for!

• You may want to complete many activities on your own, but there are some better tackled by a team of girls from your troop or group.

• Shortcuts only shortchange you. Bending the rules or taking the easy way out may earn you a recognition quickly, but will deprive you of a high-quality learning experience.

• Focus on quality, not quantity. Earning the most recognitions within your troop or group does not make you a better Girl Scout.

• Encourage and accept adult guidance when pursuing recognition work. The adult may be your leader, parent or guardian, teacher, religious leader, a community member, or a person with knowledge or training in the area you are pursuing. Your adult partner can provide thoughtful input, help you with puzzling questions, or direct you to additional resources. She or he should initial requirements as you complete them.

• Keep a record of the work you complete. The skills you acquire and the contacts you make may be useful when applying for a job or to school. Save journal entries, photographs, copies of letters you wrote or received, names and telephone numbers of people you've come in contact with, notes from oral presentations, and audio or video recordings.

• No double-dipping—work completed for one recognition requirement may not be applied to others. For example, the service you provide in your Silver Award project may not be applied to the 25-hour commitment for a Community Service bar.

With these tips in mind, plunge right in. So many exciting opportunities await you as a Cadette Girl Scout, the sooner you begin, the sooner you'll enjoy them.

INTEREST PROJECT PATCHES

Interest projects are designed to help you learn new skills or improve on the skills you already have. By the time you have completed the requirements for a particular project, you will be able to demonstrate proficiency in that area.

You can also design your own interest project or activities for existing interest projects. Consult *Cadette and Senior Girl Scout Interest Projects* for a list of interest projects and information about designing your own interest projects.

FROM DREAMS TO REALITY PATCH

To earn this recognition, which is one of the requirements for the Cadette Girl Scout Silver Award, select five activities from the list below.

1. Read the Career Exploration interest project in *Cadette and Senior Girl Scout Interest Projects*. Select and complete two of the activities.

2. Find out about at least five careers. Identify the type of training required and salary range.

3. Spend a day at work with someone who has a job in which you are interested. Discuss job responsibilities and note how time on the job is spent.

4. Research two fields in which women are not the majority.

5. Interview three mothers with salaried positions. Find out how they balance their jobs and families, how they came to be in their current positions, and what their future dreams are.

6. Collect several advertisements for at least three different positions that interest you. Compare the ads to get a general profile of each position.

COMMUNITY SERVICE RECOGNITIONS

COMMUNITY SERVICE BARS

You earn a community service bar after serving in an apprenticeship or training position. You are eligible to earn three types of community service bars:

The Cadette Girl Scout Community Service Bar (Light Blue)

The Senior Girl Scout Community Service Bar (as a Senior Girl Scout) (Burgundy)

The Community Service Bar for Contributions to Girl Scouting (Green)

There are two steps involved in earning any of the three community service bars:

1. Select the organization in which you would like to work; they must agree to train you for a minimum of four hours. Your council must approve of both the organization you have selected and the training that they propose.

You may check with your council or service unit for trainings that have been approved, or you can do your own research on organizations that offer opportunities. Then you must get council approval. It may be hard for you individually to find organizations that will train and make volunteer time available. Therefore, it is recommended that you approach organizations along with a supervising Girl Scout adult.

2. To earn the Cadette Girl Scout Community Service Bar, you must commit yourself to a minimum of 25 hours of service to an organization. If you choose to volunteer for the Girl Scout organization, you can receive the Community Service Bar in Girl Scouting.

You may continue your community service endeavors as a Senior Girl Scout. If you work 25 hours beyond those you worked as a Cadette Girl Scout or if you choose an entirely new project to which you commit 25 hours, you may receive the Senior Girl Scout Community Service Bar.

COMMUNITY SERVICE PROJECTS

To Help Where I Am Needed

Community service needs vary from community to community and from year to year. If you know your talents and values, you will always find a way to help.

Be sensitive to the world around you and the issues that concern you. You can help with:

- Homelessness
- Animal welfare
- Substance abuse
- Children in crisis

- Illiteracy
- Poverty
- Loneliness
- Unemployment

- Crime and violence
- Prejudice
- Hunger
- Pollution

Planning the Community Service Project

Beginning a community service project can seem like a big task. Use the steps below to help you choose a service project that will earn you the Cadette Girl Scout Community Service Bar:

1. IDENTIFY PROBLEMS THAT EXIST IN YOUR COMMUNITY.

   Talk to friends, neighbors, teachers, and religious leaders about community concerns.

   Read the local newspaper to see if there are problems or issues that get a lot of attention.

   Find out about the kinds of problems other community organizations are working on.

2. EVALUATE THE PRACTICAL ASPECTS OF THE PROJECT YOU WOULD LIKE TO CHOOSE.

   Will the project cost anything to carry out?

   How will you get to the meeting place?

   Are there safety issues you need to consider?

3. MAKE A COMMITMENT TO YOUR PROJECT.

   Work with a Girl Scout adult to formalize your plans for the project.

   Establish timelines and work the project into your schedule.

   Arrange for transportation.

4. BEGIN YOUR PROJECT.

In a survey of 1,400 twelve- to seventeen-year-olds, it was found that over 60 percent volunteer at least three hours a week. The top three volunteer jobs reported were baby-sitting, helping the elderly, and working in a theater or arts organization.

Sample Community Service Projects

The following list gives examples of community service projects that you might want to try. You should, however, use your imagination and creativity to develop a project that will be especially meaningful to you and your community.

Math, Science, and Technology Projects
These projects could include:

> Leading activities at a science museum.
>
> Doing computer graphics for a youth center newsletter.
>
> Counting birds for a research study.

Health and Fitness Projects
These projects could include:

> Leading an exercise class for senior citizens.
>
> Doing peer counseling at school.
>
> Volunteering for a health organization.
>
> Doing enrichment projects with children at a women's shelter.

Cultural Awareness Projects
These projects could include:

> Working at a community visitors' bureau.
>
> Working in the public library.
>
> Tutoring immigrants for citizenship exams.

Arts and Humanities Projects
These projects could include:

> Painting public murals.
>
> Working with a group to dramatize the dangers of drugs.
>
> Teaching ethnic dances at a community center.

Natural Surroundings/Camping Projects
These projects could include:

> Testing water quality for a state environmental program.
>
> Raising a guide dog.
>
> Working at a recycling station.

Girl Scouting Projects
These projects could include:

> Helping with a council newsletter.
>
> Maintaining trails at camp.
>
> Leading songs at a councilwide event.

LEADERSHIP RECOGNITIONS

CADETTE GIRL SCOUT PROGRAM AIDE

As a Cadette Girl Scout program aide, you work directly with younger girls under the supervision of an adult volunteer or staff member. Being a program aide gives you an opportunity to share your expertise and knowledge of Girl Scouting with others. After you have completed your training, you will receive a Cadette Girl Scout program aide pin, and after you have given 25 hours of service, you will receive a program aide patch. See pages 39–40 for more about becoming a Cadette Girl Scout program aide.

CADETTE GIRL SCOUT LEADERSHIP AWARD

The Cadette Girl Scout Leadership Award requires you to participate in experiences that strengthen leadership skills. Earning this recognition is a two-step process. First, you must:

• Read about leadership in Chapter 2 of this handbook.

• Complete the leadership inventory activity in the Leadership interest project in *Cadette and Senior Girl Scout Interest Projects*.

Second, you must put your knowledge of leadership to work. After you complete the above requirements, you must demonstrate leadership skills in two or more settings. Some suggestions for leadership projects are:

• Serve a term as an officer in a group.

• Assist in the leadership of younger children.

• Take charge of planning a group trip or special event.

• Complete a long-range planning calendar for your troop or group. See page 43 for help.

• Shadow or work with an adult in a leadership position. Discuss the leadership skills she uses in her job and how your experiences can help you build these skills.

Your leadership experience must total at least 25 hours. No matter how you divide the 25 hours, you must spend at least three hours on any given project. For example, you may choose to spend 17 hours arranging a trip for a group of younger girls and eight hours working with an adult who has a position of leadership. On the other hand, it would not fulfill the requirements if you spent one hour assisting younger girls, two hours planning a trip, and 22 hours working as the leader of the group because you did not spend at least three hours on the first two projects. Also, you can work for more than 25 hours.

Finally, keep a log of your leadership experience and evaluate your own leadership abilities.

Cadette Girl Scout Program Aide pin

Cadette Girl Scout Program Aide patch

Cadette Girl Scout Leadership Award pin

CADETTE GIRL SCOUT CHALLENGE

Cadette Girl Scout Challenge pin

As a Girl Scout, you are challenged to be the best possible person you can be. This involves knowing yourself, relating to others, developing values, contributing to your community, and knowing about Girl Scouting. These five areas form the basis of the Cadette Girl Scout Challenge. You complete the Challenge by doing activities from each area or section. The sections may be done in any order, though following in sequence is recommended. You may work by yourself or with others and on several sections at one time. Discuss each section and the "Wrap-Up" questions with your leader or other adult adviser.

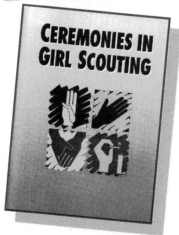

SECTION 1
KNOWING MYSELF BETTER

Challenge: Select **one** of the following activities, or design one of your own, that helps you learn more about yourself.

• Select and complete two activities from Chapter 3.

• Make a list of qualities you value in a friend. Check off the qualities you own. Of the other qualities, choose one or two you would like to have. Over a three- to four-week period, work at making these qualities your own.

• Try something new: an activity, sport, instrument, way of cooking, etc. See Chapter 6 for suggestions. Seek out someone who could help you learn the new skill. Spend at least five hours learning this skill.

• Try two or more activities from the Fashion/Fitness/Makeup interest project in *Cadette and Senior Girl Scout Interest Projects* to enhance your appearance.

SECTION 2

RELATING TO OTHERS BETTER

Challenge: Do **one** of the activities below, or design your own "relating" activity.

• Select and complete two activities from Chapter 4.

• Plan and carry out an outing or party for a family, hospital patients, senior citizens, or a group in your community.

• Plan and carry out a co-ed event, such as a day of sports or backpacking, a debate, or a party. Include boys on the planning committee.

SECTION 3

DEVELOPING VALUES FOR LIVING

Challenge: Do at least **one** of the following activities:

• Read the section "Your Values" in Chapter 3. Do the activity on exploring your attitudes, values, and interests on page 56, and the value rank activity on page 57.

• Read the sections on prejudice, stereotyping, and discrimination in Chapter 3. Complete the activity on page 59.

• Take an active part in planning and carrying out a Girl Scouts' Own ceremony (see page 19). It should demonstrate the ways the Girl Scout Promise and Law can help you serve God and your country and become a good citizen.

SECTION 4

CONTRIBUTING TO MY COMMUNITY

Challenge: Select **one** activity from the following list, or plan an activity of your own.

• Organize a children's sports day, assist at a community fair, or become involved with the work of a well-known organization (for example, the Special Olympics).

• Become a literacy or library volunteer, help conduct programs for immigrants, assist with voting campaigns, organize anti-drug efforts, or educate community members about childhood immunizations.

• Serve as an audiovisual assistant in your school, troop, council, or religious organization.

• Become a volunteer math or science tutor.

• Teach arts and crafts to children, senior citizens, or hospital patients.

• Demonstrate water safety for children, help repair and maintain your council's small craft, or assist in a water-conservation project.

SECTION 5

KNOWING ABOUT GIRL SCOUTING

Challenge: Select **one** of the following activities or design one of your own that shows you have knowledge of Girl Scouting, its purpose, and its history.

• Read about Juliette Low in Chapter 1. Talk about her life to the girls in your troop or another audience, possibly a group of younger girls.

• Design an activity that will help others learn more about Girl Scouting and WAGGGS.

• Prepare a booklet or presentation for younger girls that describes at least two countries, other than the United States, in which there are members of the World Association. *Trefoil Round the World* is a useful reference book about Girl Scouting and Girl Guiding.

• Write a biography, poems or songs, a short story, or a play about Girl Scouting.

• Accompany a Girl Scout council staff member, camp staff person, or volunteer for a few hours to explore career possibilities in Girl Scouting.

• Learn about ways to volunteer in Girl Scouting or volunteer to work at your Girl Scout council office.

• Assist in your council's efforts to attract new members to Girl Scouting.

WRAP-UP

When you have completed all five sections of the Cadette Girl Scout Challenge, ask yourself the following questions. Then discuss your thoughts and ideas with your leader or troop or group.

1. What did you learn about yourself?

_____

_____

_____

2. How did your Challenge work affect others?

_____

_____

_____

3. How did you apply your talents?

_____

_____

_____

4. How do your accomplishments relate to the ideals of Girl Scouting?

_____

_____

_____

5. How would you improve what you did?

_____

_____

_____

6. How will the things you learned help you in the future?

_____

_____

_____

GIRL SCOUT SILVER AWARD

This is the highest award you can earn as a Cadette Girl Scout. It recognizes your efforts in a range of Girl Scout and community experiences as well as your commitment to working to better your life and the lives of others.

The first four requirements of the award ask you to build your skills, explore career possibilities, increase your leadership skills, and make a commitment to improving yourself. You can do them in any order, but they must be completed prior to the fifth requirement, the Girl Scout Silver Award Project. You should work closely with your adult adviser in the completion of all the requirements.

Review *Safety-Wise* and council guidelines on activities you can participate in as a Girl Scout, particularly those related to fund raising. If you plan to work with other girls on Silver Award activities, remember that each girl must have specific responsibilities that allow her to learn and grow. Requirements begun prior to being a registered Cadette Girl Scout may not be applied to this award.

REQUIREMENTS

1. Earn three interest project patches related to the project you will do for the Silver Award. It is important that the interest projects you choose

The Cadette Girl Scout Silver Award

correspond to your goals for the Silver Award. It does not matter, however, when you actually completed a particular interest project (provided you were a registered Cadette Girl Scout). You should work closely with your Silver Award adviser to determine which interest projects correspond to your Silver Award.

2. Earn the From Dreams to Reality patch or Career Exploration Interest patch.

3. Earn the Cadette Girl Scout Leadership Award or Leadership Interest Project patch.

4. Earn the Cadette Girl Scout Challenge.

5. Design and carry out a Girl Scout Silver Award project.

Earning the Girl Scout Silver Award

The four quarters of the inner circle represent the first four requirements you must complete when earning the Girl Scout Silver Award. The outer circle, the Girl Scout Silver Award Project, is the final requirement you must complete to earn the Silver Award.

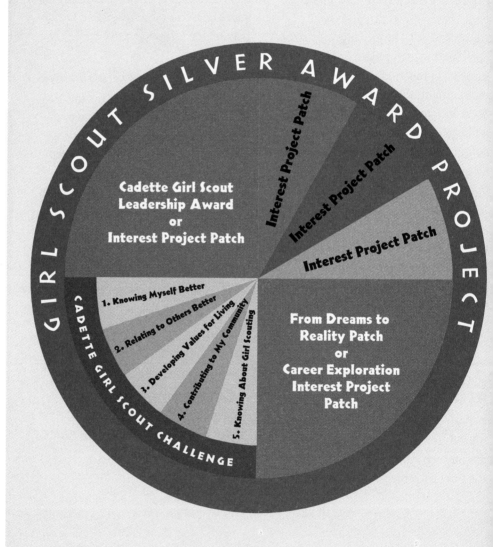

THE GIRL SCOUT SILVER AWARD PROJECT

This project builds upon your accomplishments in Girl Scouting and represents your personal action plan for helping others. The project could be done in or outside of Girl Scouting and must reflect some aspect of community service. If the project is done within Girl Scouting, you must reach out to the community in some way—for example, by calling on people outside Girl Scouts as resources, doing something that reaches girls who aren't Girl Scouts, or affecting something that is used by people other than just Girl Scouts.

The Silver Award project has five steps. Your project, including planning and execution, should take a minimum of 30 hours. The actual implementation of the project should take from 7 to 10 hours. Obtain a copy of the Cadette Girl Scout Silver Award Report Form from your council office to keep a record of your Silver Award work. Fill it out completely and keep a copy for yourself and your adviser.

Review *Safety-Wise* for do's and don'ts. You should work with your Girl Scout council on any project that will impact Girl Scouting or Girl Scout property. As with any other project, you must have approval if you plan to raise funds or solicit donations.

The following steps will help you organize and carry out the Girl Scout Silver Award project:

STEP 1:   **Decide which values, experience, and skills you would like to put into action through the Silver Award project.**

STEP 2:   **Decide on a project that will use your personal strengths to help others. You can work with your school, the community, a religious group, or Girl Scouting. (See "Sample Girl Scout Silver Award Projects" below.)**

STEP 3:   **Identify the people with whom you will work: Those who will help and guide you, those who will work with you, those whom you hope to help. Be sure to include a Girl Scout leader or another adult from your council.**

STEP 4:   **Create a timeline and a budget, if necessary. If you work with a group, divide jobs and set up a way to ensure that everyone is on track.**

STEP 5:   **Carry out your plan. This final step of your project should total at least seven hours. This may be done all on one day or divided into segments. When you have completed your project, write a brief evaluation. Share the evaluation with your adviser and council representative.**

SAMPLE GIRL SCOUT SILVER AWARD PROJECTS

• A Cadette Girl Scout troop planned a week-long literacy celebration at their local library. They arranged for local celebrities to host story hours, held a panel discussion of teen books, and put on a play that featured favorite book characters.

• A Cadette Girl Scout decided the camp library needed updating. She made a list of books and games needed and asked each troop in her service unit to contribute an item on her list. She then catalogued the items and devised a checkout system.

• Six Cadette Girl Scouts coordinated an effort to help their local food pantry restock its shelves after a community crisis. They designed posters and fliers to promote the effort and got supermarkets and theaters to help sponsor the "can-a-thon." The girls decorated "donation barrels" from the local moving company and worked with the fire department to arrange food pick-ups.

• A Cadette Girl Scout troop wrote and put on a play about self-esteem for girls in low-income housing areas.

• A Cadette Girl Scout campaigned to get a traffic light installed at a busy intersection in her community. Her work entailed researching accidents, gathering testimony from residents and police, circulating a petition, and attending city council meetings.

OTHER RECOGNITIONS

AMERICAN INDIAN YOUTH CERTIFICATE AND YOUTH AWARD SILVER MEDALLION

Any registered Girl Scout age 12 through 17 may earn the American Indian Youth Certificate and attend the annual American Indian Girl Scouting/Boy Scouting Seminar. Furthermore, girls who are of American Indian descent, who have met the requirements for the certificate, and have attended the annual seminar are eligible to compete for the American Indian Youth Award Silver Medallion.

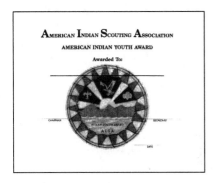

If you are interested in earning this award, consult GSUSA's Council Service Publication *American Indian Youth Certificate and Award* for current requirements. Requirements change periodically, so write to Girl Scouts of the U.S.A., 420 Fifth Avenue, New York, N.Y. 10018 for a free copy of the most current publication.

RELIGIOUS RECOGNITIONS

Religious recognitions have been developed nationally by individual religious groups so that a girl might learn more about her faith and become a stronger member of her religious group. Work with your clergy or youth adviser to pursue the recognition in your community, or use the chart to contact your national group for further information.

GIRL SCOUTS

G is for the girl inside of me just waiting to explore
All the wonderful experiences in life I have in store
I is for the interest that I exhibit with each new task
Wondering how it is possible that the next one
will be better than the last
R is for the richness that I feel inside
As I walk through life with my parents
and my brother by my side
L is for the lady inside of me just waiting to come out
While the child inside of me is still learning
what life is all about
S is for the Girl Scout in me
who always wants to know more
Scouting has given me many new
opportunities to explore
C is for the campfire with its tall flames burning bright
As we sing the song of memories
before we say Good-Night
O is for the World of Out-of-Doors
that is so much a part of me
Scouting has helped me appreciate everything I see
U is for the unexpected things I'll encounter in my life
Some I might be thankful for, others I might not like
T is for the thanks I give to people who have cared
It's with them that memories are made
and special thoughts are shared

–Alicia Brillo, age 15,
Plymouth Bay Girl Scout Council,
Massachusetts

Religious Recognitions

Religious Group	Cadette Girl Scout Recognition	Ages
Baha'i	Unity of Mankind	
Buddhist	Padma Award	Ages 12-14
Christian Science	Christian Science God and Country	Ages 11-14
Eastern Orthodox	Alpha Omega	Ages 11-14
Episcopal	God and Church	Ages 11-14 Grades 6-9
Islamic	Quratula'in Award	Ages 12-15
Jewish	Menorah Award	Ages 11-14
Lutheran	God and Church	Ages 11-13, Grades 6-8
(Mormon) Church of Jesus Christ of Latter-Day Saints	Young Woman of Truth	Ages 12-13
Protestant and Independent Christian Churches	God and Church God and Life	Ages 11-13, Grades 6-8 Ages 14-17 Grades 9-12
Reorganized Church of Jesus Christ of Latter Day Saints	Liahona	Ages 12-14
Roman Catholic Church	Marian Medal	Ages 12-14
(Quakers) Society of Friends	Spirit of Truth	Ages 11-14, Grades 6-9
Unitarian Universalist	Religion in Life	Ages 12-14
Unity Church	Light of God	Ages 11-13

* For further information see *Religious Recognitions for Girls and Adults in Girl Scouting,* CSP 40-153-340, available from Council Service Publications, Girl Scouts of the U.S.A., 420 Fifth Avenue, New York, N.Y. 10018-2702

Placement of Girl Scout Insignia and Recognitions

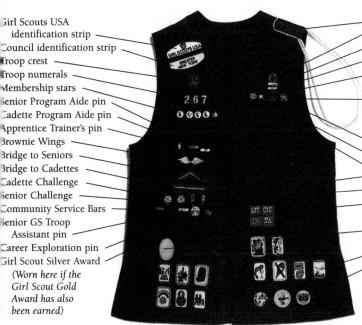

Girl Scouts USA identification strip

Council identification strip

Troop crest

Troop numerals

Membership stars

Senior Program Aide pin

Cadette Program Aide pin

Apprentice Trainer's pin

Brownie Wings

Bridge to Seniors

Bridge to Cadettes

Cadette Challenge

Senior Challenge

Community Service Bars

Senior GS Troop Assistant pin

Career Exploration pin

Girl Scout Silver Award
(Worn here if the Girl Scout Gold Award has also been earned)

Patrol leader's cord

World Trefoil pin

CIT II pin

LIT/CIT project pins

Girl Scout membership pin

Girl Scout Silver Award (only worn here if this is highest award earned)

Girl Scout Gold Award

Numeral guard

Ten-Year Award

Cadette Leadership Award

Senior Leadership Award

LIT/CIT and Program Aide patches

From Dreams to Reality patch

Interest project patches

Tan proficiency badges earned as a Cadette

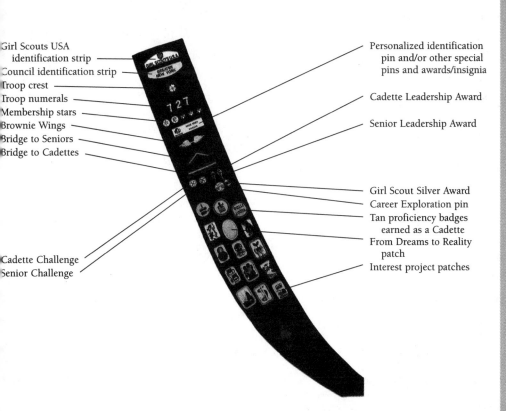

Girl Scouts USA identification strip

Council identification strip

Troop crest

Troop numerals

Membership stars

Brownie Wings

Bridge to Seniors

Bridge to Cadettes

Cadette Challenge

Senior Challenge

Personalized identification pin and/or other special pins and awards/insignia

Cadette Leadership Award

Senior Leadership Award

Girl Scout Silver Award

Career Exploration pin

Tan proficiency badges earned as a Cadette

From Dreams to Reality patch

Interest project patches

BRIDGE TO SENIOR GIRL SCOUTS PATCH

Moving from one Girl Scout age level to the next is called bridging. To earn the Bridge to Senior Girl Scouts patch, complete the following eight steps in your last year of Cadette Girl Scouting.

1. Find out about Senior Girl Scouting. Interview at least two former or current Senior Girl Scouts to find out what they do at this age level.

2. Page through *A Resource Book for Senior Girl Scouts* to learn more about Senior Girl Scouting. Read two sections from two different chapters in that book.

3. Do something with a Senior Girl Scout. You might visit a Senior Girl Scout meeting or help out with an interest or community service project.

4. Help others learn about Cadette and/or Senior Girl Scouting.

5. Find out more about Apprentice Trainer, Leader-in-Training (LIT), and Counselor-in-Training (CIT) opportunities available in your area. Review a *Wider Ops* magazine to see which opportunities are open to Senior Girl Scouts only.

6. Conduct a leadership activity with a group of younger Girl Scouts.

7. Design your own bridging ceremony. Consult the GSUSA resource, *Ceremonies in Girl Scouting*, for ideas.

8. Plan and participate in a summer Girl Scout activity.

THE END OF A NEW FREEDOM

*Like a river, life twists and turns
through the hours.
Changing speeds to accomplish goals
and opportunities.
Like a river, life rises and falls
through hard and easy times
Being polluted as life can be
polluted with harm and danger.
Like a river, life can be used
to gain and produce,
Expanding and narrowing
to fit into tasks.
As the river slows, it becomes
frail and gentle.
Like life, the water is still at the end
laid to rest,
to go wherever it feels free.*

–Hillary Thompson, age 16,
Great Rivers Girl Scout Council,
Ohio

INDEX